CHRIST IN THE WILDERNESS

STUDIES IN BIBLICAL THEOLOGY

CHRIST IN THE WILDERNESS

*The Wilderness Theme in the Second Gospel
and its Basis in the Biblical Tradition*

ULRICH MAUSER

WIPF & STOCK · Eugene, Oregon

Wipf and Stock Publishers
199 W 8th Ave, Suite 3
Eugene, OR 97401

Christ in the Wilderness
By Mauser, Ulrich W.
Copyright©1963 SCM Press
ISBN 13: 978-1-60899-021-4
Publication date 9/15/2009
Previously published by SCM Press, 1963

Copyright © SCM Press 1963
First English edition 1963 by SCM Press
This Edition published by arrangement with SCM-Canterbury Press

CONTENTS

Preface	7
Abbreviations	9
I. INTRODUCTION	11
II. ISRAEL IN THE WILDERNESS	15
1. Importance and extent of the wilderness tradition in the Old Testament	15
2. Linguistic evidence in the Masoretic text and in the Septuagint	18
3. The role of the desert in the historical accounts of the Pentateuch	20
4. The wilderness in the Psalms and Prophets	36
III. THE TIME BETWEEN THE TESTAMENTS	53
1. Philo of Alexandria	53
2. Apocalyptic and pseudepigraphic literature	54
3. The Rabbis	55
4. Josephus	56
5. The community of Qumran	58
IV. THE WILDERNESS THEME IN THE NEW TESTAMENT	62
1. Pauline epistles	63
2. Acts	68
3. Hebrews	72
4. The Fourth Gospel	75
V. THE PROLOGUE OF MARK	77
1. Literary and thematic unity of 1.1–13	77
2. The Prophecy	80
3. The Herald	82
4. The Lord	89

Contents

VI. THE WAY THROUGH THE DESERT 103
    1. Introductory considerations 103
    2. Formal characteristics and correlations of the wilderness passages 105
    3. The mountain 108
    4. The phrase κατ' ἰδίαν and the parables 119
    5. The sea 124
    6. Temptation 128
    7. The followers 132
    8. Conclusions 138

VII. THE WILDERNESS IN MATTHEW AND LUKE 144
    1. Matthew 144
    2. Luke 146

Index of Authors 151

Index of References 154

PREFACE

THE ideas expressed in this book have grown out of Bible studies on the Gospel of Mark in which my friend, Dr Daniel B. Wessler, and I were engaged for an hour every morning while we were still fellow workers in the campus ministry at Oregon State University. I take this opportunity to thank my generous friend for the enrichment and inspiration which I was privileged to enjoy through our work and studies together.

The following pages would not have their present form had it not been for the help of several scholars who had the kindness to read my manuscript, partly as a rough draft and partly in a considerably revised form. Professor Floyd V. Filson, Dr A. R. C. Leaney and Professors C. F. D. Moule and G. Ernest Wright from the staff of the Advisory Editors of this series have given me many helpful criticisms and suggestions, for which I wish to express my sincere thanks. Professors Markus Barth and James M. Robinson have commented extensively on a first draft of this book, for which I am greatly indebted to them. Dr Leslie Zeigler of the Department of Philosophy and Religion at Oregon State University has taken great pains to eradicate a good many Germanisms in my writing. Her help in this, as well as her never-failing encouragement, have been invaluable. To my secretary, Mrs N. McKeehan, who typed my manuscript, I owe my thanks.

Corvallis, Oregon ULRICH MAUSER
June 1962

ABBREVIATIONS

ATD	Das Alte Testament Deutsch
BK	Biblischer Kommentar: Altes Testament
BKW	Bible Key Words
HUCA	*Hebrew Union College Annual*
ICC	International Critical Commentary
JBL	*Journal of Biblical Literature*
JBR	*Journal of Bible and Religion*
JEH	*Journal of Ecclesiastical History*
RB	*Revue Biblique*
SBT	Studies in Biblical Theology
SJT	*Scottish Journal of Theology*
ZAW	*Zeitschrift für die alttestamentliche Wissenschaft*
ZNW	*Zeitschrift für die neutestamentliche Wissenschaft*
ZTK	*Zeitschrift für Theologie und Kirche*

I

INTRODUCTION

In the years following the First World War a new approach toward the understanding of the New Testament literature was advanced by a number of German-speaking scholars. The new method had grown out of the literary criticism of the Gospels and became widely known by the name of Form-Criticism. Martin Dibelius,[1] K. L. Schmidt[2] and R. Bultmann[3] were the pioneers of this approach, which has ever since exercised a decisive influence on New Testament scholarship, at least on the European continent. A good number of English-speaking scholars have also, to a greater or lesser degree, recognized the validity of this method and in their own work contributed to its advancement.[4] The work of the pioneers mentioned, along with a great deal of subsequent research carried out by a large group of scholars, seems to have established beyond doubt several results. Our Synoptic Gospels are collections of numerous pieces of tradition about Jesus' life and teaching. These stories were, to a large extent, independent little units originally quite unrelated to each other, as they were preserved by the oral tradition of the Church. Prior to their incorporation in the Synoptic Gospels they had already undergone some transformation—the traditions had a tendency to grow, single sayings were arranged to form a chain of logia, some sayings were embedded in stories about the life of Christ, and some groups of stories had already been

---

[1] Martin Dibelius, *Die Formgeschichte des Evangeliums*, 1st ed., 1919. Quoted according to the English translation of the 2nd ed. by B. L. Woolf, *From Tradition to Gospel*, 1935.
[2] K. L. Schmidt, *Der Rahmen der Geschichte Jesu*, 1919.
[3] R. Bultmann, *Die Geschichte der synoptischen Tradition*, 1st ed., 1921.
[4] See, e.g., F. C. Grant, *The Growth of the Gospels*, 1933; V. Taylor, *The Formation of the Gospel Tradition*, 1933; C. H. Dodd, *The Apostolic Preaching and its Developments*, 1936; R. H. Lightfoot, *Locality and Doctrine in the Gospels*, 1938; E. B. Redlich, *Form Criticism, its Value and Limitations*, 1939; L. T. McGinley, *Form-Criticism of the Synoptic Healing Narratives*, 1944.

Introduction

incorporated into a continuous unit. When these traditions were linked together in a Gospel, as far as we know for the first time by Mark, they already existed in certain literary forms. The arrangement of the segments of the Gospel tradition into a continuous story was the work of the Evangelists and the motives prompting the arrangement were theological, catechetical and homiletical rather than historical. Form-critics themselves, it is true, are in disagreement as to what precisely was the character of these forms and what were the motives which caused their formation. Much research still needs to be done to further clarify our understanding. But the fact appears to be certain that the Evangelists used materials which had already been formed in the process of oral tradition.

During the last decade, however, it was realized that a step beyond form-criticism was necessary. Form-critics regarded the Evangelists purely as collectors of traditional material which had already been shaped. Martin Dibelius may be quoted as typical in this respect. He writes: 'The literary understanding of the synoptics begins with the recognition that they are collections of material. The composers are only to the smallest extent authors. They are principally collectors, vehicles of tradition, editors.'[1] Beginning with that assumption, it was regarded as an exegetical principle to interpret each literary unit in the Synoptics on its own merits. Since the links between the pericopae were historically secondary, form-critical exegesis tended to deal with the text primarily in small sections and to disregard the links as of less importance. In this respect an important change has taken place. On the basis of the results of form-criticism, it has become apparent that all Evangelists were more than simple collectors. They were collectors, it is true, but their way of relating the tradition was highly significant. Theological motives were at work in the manner of arrangement and thus each of the Synoptic Gospels is a unity, well calculated and thoroughly planned. Each Gospel in its entirety has a certain kerygmatic intention which gives it its own particular character. In view of this, scholars have recently attempted to sketch the characteristic intentions of the various Evangelists by taking seriously the framework into which they moulded the tradition as it was available to them. In such

[1] Martin Dibelius, *Tradition*, p. 3.

Introduction

study, the redactor's work is not of secondary, but of primary importance. The ways in which stories and sayings were grouped together, the remarks concerning localities and dates, and, most important of all, the continuity of the account as envisaged by the Evangelists, are of supreme weight. Only by taking into account the creative intentions of the Evangelists can an adequate understanding of their message as a whole be achieved. This type of research has produced a number of monographs related to each of the Synoptic Gospels. H. Conzelmann's, *Die Mitte der Zeit. Studien zur Theologie des Lukas,* 1957[1], concerning Luke, and the symposium[2] by Barth, Bornkamm and Held, *Überlieferung und Auslegung im Matthäus-Evangelium,* 1959, concerning Matthew, may be mentioned. With regard to Mark, a book by W. Marxsen, *Der Evangelist Markus. Studien zur Redaktionsgeschichte des Evangeliums,* 2nd ed., 1959, pursues the same purpose.

This type of research endeavouring to reveal the kerygmatic intentions of the Evangelists has found a helpful ally in the discovery of certain themes which are woven into the redactionary framework of the Synoptics rather than in the older tradition itself. Conzelmann has pointed out that a certain understanding of Christ's place in history is the dominant factor in Luke and forms the backbone of his composition. In Mark's Gospel, E. Lohmeyer had drawn attention to the theme of Galilee which runs through the whole narrative.[3] This observation serves as a starting-point for the work of W. Marxsen, mentioned above.

In the present enquiry an attempt is made to trace some of the characteristics of Mark's Gospel, using the theme of the wilderness as a guide. At first glance the wilderness theme does not seem to be very illuminating for a study of the distinctive nature of the second Evangelist; neither are the references to the wilderness very plentiful, nor does there appear to be much difference from the accounts given by the other two Synoptics. However, I hope to show that these objections are not valid and that Mark used traditions about the wilderness in a way both peculiar to him and highly significant for his theology.

The land in which Jesus lived was, and is, a land comprising

---

[1] English translation, *The Theology of St Luke,* 1960, by Geoffrey Buswell.
[2] ET, *Tradition and Interpretation in Matthew,* 1963.
[3] E. Lohmeyer, *Galiläa und Jerusalem,* 1936.

Introduction

desert areas. It is therefore not surprising to find references to the wilderness in many books of the Old and New Testaments. Although there are several remarks concerning the wilderness in the New Testament which simply reflect the natural conditions of the land in Palestine, they are remarkably rare. In the majority of the cases, whenever the wilderness is mentioned, the thought of the New Testament writer is not directed to the geographical disposition of the country, but to the memory of the basic action of God which took place in the wilderness in the course of Israel's history. The long series of all-important events which happened to her from the time of her delivery out of Egyptian bondage to the settlement of the tribes in Canaan has by no means become irrelevant to the congregations of the New Covenant. The Church of the New Testament understands herself as the legitimate heir of Israel. Hence the tradition of the sojourn in the desert is part of her own heritage and, consequently, the New Testament writers refer mainly to Israel's exodus when they talk about the wilderness. Ἔρημος is, therefore, primarily used as an absolute noun needing no specifying attribute; it is not a certain locality on the map of the Middle East, but the place of God's mighty acts, significant for all believers of all times and places. Since, in recalling God's action with Israel in the wilderness, the New Testament refers to the accounts of the Old Testament, it is necessary for us, first of all, to outline the desert tradition in the Old Testament.

II

ISRAEL IN THE WILDERNESS

1. IMPORTANCE AND EXTENT OF THE WILDERNESS TRADITION IN THE OLD TESTAMENT

THE narration of Israel's sojourn in the wilderness occupies large portions of the Old Testament. Major parts of Exodus and the entire books of Leviticus and Numbers in their final stage of textual tradition tell of events which are described as having happened to Israel during her life in the desert. Deuteronomy is presented as Moses' testament to his people, issued at the last station of their long and hazardous wanderings through the peninsula of Sinai on the verge of their entering the promised land (Deut. 1.1). Only small sections of the vast traditions contained in those books actually trace Israel's travels in the desert; nevertheless the desert is the common geographical setting of all the material in these parts of the Pentateuch whenever, after a long process of composition, it emerged in its final shape.

The wilderness tradition takes up a major portion of the historical books of the Old Testament, and in this tradition events of fundamental importance to the history and belief of the Israelite tribes are related to the desert locality. Basic data of Yahweh's self-disclosure to his people are given in this area—the revelation of God's name, the theophany on Mount Sinai, the establishment of the covenant with Israel, and the declaration of the law. Within certain limitations it can be said that Israel's fundamental belief in her election as God's chosen people is rooted in the wilderness tradition.[1]

The presence of very heterogeneous traditions and their setting in the general location of the wilderness appear to be the result of a systematic arrangement of traditions which were originally independent of each other. Investigations made by

---

[1] For the limitations of this statement, cf. p. 28.

Christ in the Wilderness

G. von Rad[1] and M. Noth[2] establish the fact that Israel's belief was based on a creed which preserved the fundamental events of God's unique dealings with his people out of which, in turn, evolved the whole Pentateuch as a literary work. This creed was handed down in various shorter and longer forms. Even in its most primitive form it contains at least two fixed points—the exodus from Egypt and the inheritance of the promised land (Deut. 6.21–23; 26.5–9). The deliverance from Egyptian bondage is the central point of Israelite faith.[3] Thus Hosea, insisting upon the basic foundation of Israel's existence over against the corruption of her religion through the worship of Canaanite deities, was able to coin the expression, 'Yahweh, your God from the land of Egypt' (Hos. 12.9; 13.4; cf. 11.1). The time between the exodus and the conquest of Canaan is omitted in the most rudimentary forms of the creed. Stories about the events during the journeys of the tribes which, according to M. Noth,[4] were originally handed down independently of the exodus tradition, were, however, at some very early stage in the formation of the Pentateuch introduced between the narratives about the Egyptian liberation and the conquest of Canaan. Accordingly, we find a more elaborate form of the basic Israelite creed which includes the sojourn in the wilderness, e.g. Josh. 24.2–13. This stage of the tradition is the presupposition for the numerous allusions to the wilderness period in all parts of the Old Testament. By the time of the eighth-century prophets the themes of the exodus from Egypt and the wanderings in the wilderness have already become an indissoluble unit. Amos 9.7 looks as though Amos knew only the deliverance from Egypt. But Amos 2.10 proves the intimate correlation of the themes in the mind of the prophet. Hosea, likewise, gives the impression in some passages that he regards the exodus alone as the primary element of Yahwistic religion.[5] But apart from the significant use of the wilderness theme in other passages, with which we will be concerned later, Hos. 12.9

---

[1] Gerhard von Rad, *Das formgeschichtliche Problem des Hexateuchs*, 1938 [also in *Gesammelte Studien zum AT*, 1957].

[2] Martin Noth, *Überlieferungsgeschichte des Pentateuchs*, 1948.

[3] G. Ernest Wright, *The Old Testament against its environment* (SBT, 2), 1950, pp. 49 f.

[4] Martin Noth, *Überlieferungsgeschichte des Pentateuch*.

[5] See Hos. 11.1; 12.9; 13.4, quoted above.

Israel in the Wilderness

establishes a very close connexion of the themes—Yahweh, the God from the land of Egypt, will make Israel dwell again in tents, an obvious allusion to the life in the wilderness. The fusion of the exodus story with elements of the desert tradition is equally clear in Micah 6.4 f. From this time on both themes are generally regarded as a coherent whole and as such they are used by most of the great prophets[1] and in several psalms.[2]

It is worth noticing, moreover, that in several instances we find passages which seem to indicate that the wilderness period was the decisive phase in Israel's primeval history. A verse like Hos. 9.10: 'Like grapes in the wilderness I found Israel' appears to betray a certain amount of divergency from the usual concept that Israel was called into being by the liberation from the Egyptian captivity. Ezek. 16.5[3] and Jer. 31.2 show, although less clearly, a similar understanding of God's initial action with his people and Deut. 32.10 states the same conception. However, these isolated passages are insufficient ground to postulate the existence of a tradition in some Israelite groups which saw in the wilderness period the proper beginning of Israel's election.[4] It is probably safer to assume that at least since the eighth century the themes of the exodus and the wilderness were so thoroughly amalgamated that whenever either of them was mentioned the association of the other was covertly implied.

The attempt will not be made in the following pages to delineate methodically the development of Israel's thought concerning the wilderness. This would involve a thorough historical treatment of all available evidence. The primary concern of our study is the Second Gospel, and it is needless to emphasize that the authors of the New Testament period did not read the Old Testament with the eyes of the modern critic. We are concerned here not with the intricacies of the historical process of thought, but with the deposit of motifs which were stored in the desert tradition of the Old

---

[1] Isaiah is a notable exception. An allusion may, however, be found in Isa. 1.2.

[2] Some psalms which recapitulate Israel's history contain only scanty recollections of the wilderness episodes, e.g. Ps. 105. The significance of this fact will be discussed below, pp. 37 ff.

[3] The phrase 'you were cast out on the open field', Ezek. 16.5, is likely to refer to the time in the desert: W. Zimmerli, *Ezechiel* (BK), p. 345.

[4] This thesis has been advanced by R. Bach, *Die Erwählung Israels in der Wüste*, Diss. Bonn. 1951 (unpublished dissertation).

Testament and which may prove to be fertile for the theology of the primitive Church. Our approach will, therefore, not be historical, following the chronological order of the Old Testament writings, but rather topical, tracing the main ideas which are sometimes preserved only in certain strata of the texts and sometimes maintained from the most ancient to the most recent elements of the tradition.

2. LINGUISTIC EVIDENCE IN THE MASORETIC TEXT AND IN THE SEPTUAGINT

The word ἔρημος is used by the LXX both as a noun and as an adjective to translate a variety of Hebrew roots and their derivations. Four of these Hebrew words have to be more closely examined: מִדְבָּר, שְׁמָמָה, חָרְבָּה, עֲרָבָה. Of these words, מִדְבָּר is used much more frequently than any other term denoting wilderness. Furthermore, and this is important for us, the noun ἡ ἔρημος is firmly tied to מִדְבָּר. Also, the LXX renders בַּמִּדְבָּר (in the desert) commonly with ἐν τῇ ἐρήμῳ or εἰς τὴν ἔρημον.[1] In the Pentateuch, מִדְבָּר, and consequently ἔρημος in the LXX, is almost exclusively applied with reference to the wilderness of the sojourn. In the former prophets the word carries the same connotation as in the Pentateuch, but it is now also applied to areas in or adjacent to Palestine proper. In the latter prophets still another use of מִדְבָּר (ἔρημος) can be discerned. While the application to the wilderness of the sojourn is retained the term is now widely employed in contexts which reveal strong associations with mythology common to the peoples of the Near East.[2]

מִדְבָּר is derived from the root דבר, the original meaning of which is to drive.[3] מִדְבָּר thus connotes the place where the cattle are driven. This makes it clear that the word does not necessarily convey the meaning of a sand desert with absolutely no vegetation, rather it means sparsely inhabited, barren plains which, however, provide enough pasturage for herds.

While the meaning of מִדְבָּר arose from the everyday life of the

[1] Werner Schmauch, *Orte der Offenbarung and der Offenbarungsort im Neuen Testament*, 1956, p. 29.
[2] Robert W. Funk, 'The Wilderness', *JBL* 78 (1959), p. 207.
[3] Wilhelm Gesenius, *Handwörterbuch über das Alte Testament*, 10th ed., 1886, p. 177b.

nomadic herdsmen, the etymology of שְׁמָמָה and חָרְבָּה gives us a glance into the psychological and mythological implications which were associated with the wilderness in the Israelite's soul. Both words combine the notion of confusion and destruction with the image of the barren land. The verbal form שמם, from which שְׁמָמָה is derived, describes the paralysis which befalls an individual, a community, or even the land itself when evil and curse touch it. The wilderness is the place where evil and curse prevail and which, therefore, is in a state of destruction causing tremor in man.[1] The same interesting double meaning can be observed in חָרְבָּה, which basically denotes destruction, but is often used in the sense of dry, arid country.[2]

עֲרָבָה in contrast with the other three words, is mainly used to signify a definite geographical area of arid character; namely, the lower Jordan valley from Jericho southwards along the shores of the Dead Sea and down to the Gulf of Aqabah.[3]

Since the nominal form of ἔρημος is in the LXX virtually tied to מִדְבָּר it might seem sufficient to restrict the present discussion to this word. But through this procedure it would be impossible to do justice to the very significant fact that in the latter prophets the four Hebrew words are often used synonymously.[4] The blend of terms which quite neutrally describe a geographic location (מִדְבָּר, עֲרָבָה) with those full of mythological and emotional meaning (חָרְבָּה, שְׁמָמָה), make up the characteristics of the latter prophets' thinking about the wilderness. This evidence actually gives an important clue for the development of Israel's reflection about her time in the desert. In the Pentateuch the emphasis is primarily on the historical account of what occurred during the forty years' sojourn. The relatively neutral word מִדְבָּר was the fit

[1] J. Pedersen, *Israel* I–II, 1926, pp. 457 f.
[2] W. Gesenius, *op. cit.*, p. 290b. James Barr (*The Semantics of Biblical Language*, 1961) has criticized the way in which etymological arguments are commonly employed, suggesting that 'the distinctiveness of Biblical thought and language has to be settled at sentence level, that is, by the things the writers say, and not by the words they say them with' (*ibid.*, p. 270). It would seem that in the case of the Hebrew words discussed above, the result of the etymological analysis is in many cases amply substantiated by the context in which the words occur, so that Barr's argument does not apply in our case.
[3] W. Gesenius, *op. cit.*, p. 653a.
[4] מִדְבָּר and שְׁמָמָה are used synonymously, e.g. Isa. 64.9; Zeph. 2.13 f.; Jer. 4.23–28. מִדְבָּר, שְׁמָמָה and חָרְבָה are synonymous in Mal. 1.3 f.

expression to fix the locality of these strange and miraculous events. In the prophets, the period of the forty years is made the object of a highly sophisticated process of theological reflection. The events of the sojourn, firmly established in Israel's creed, were not questioned as facts. But in order to work out their perennial significance the prophets chose a vocabulary which did not restrict them to a mere commemoration of the past. For this task words rich with emotional and cultural meaning could aptly be employed.

3. THE ROLE OF THE DESERT IN THE HISTORICAL ACCOUNTS OF THE PENTATEUCH

It has been mentioned before that the themes of the exodus from Egypt and of the journeys in the wilderness were originally independent traditions (cf. p. 16). However, in this section they will be treated as a homogeneous unit[1] and the cluster of stories centred round Mount Sinai will be included, although their incorporation into the continuous narrative of the Pentateuch is probably of an even later date.[2] The sequence of history as we now have it in the biblical text was, of course, seen as a whole by the time of Christ.

Within the Pentateuch itself, however, there is a noticeable difference in the treatment of the wilderness tradition. In Exodus and Numbers stories are told—most extraordinary and astonishing stories—but the thoughtfulness and astonishment of the reader is provoked by the tale as such. If there is any teaching involved, any application of a time-transcending significance intended, then it is not specifically stated. In Deuteronomy the situation is changed. A number of the wilderness stories contained in Exodus and Numbers are briefly repeated at the beginning of the book (Deut. 1.6–3.29), but the recapitulation of history only serves as a background against which the teaching of Deuteronomy stands out. The wilderness period has become the text for a sermon.[3]

[1] I shall, therefore, henceforth use the word exodus in a way which comprises the entire wanderings of Israel from the moment of their departure from Egypt to the conquest of Canaan.
[2] See Kurt Galling, *Die Erwählungstraditionen Israels* (Beihefte ZAW 48), 1928, pp. 26–37.
[3] The distinction is made by Gerhard von Rad, *Old Testament Theology* I (trans. of *Theologie des AT* I [1957], with additions), 1962, p. 288.

Israel in the Wilderness

(a) Danger and Help in the Desert

The desert stories of Exodus and Numbers almost always combine two elements: danger and divine help. The wilderness is the place that threatens the very existence of Yahweh's chosen people, but it is also the stage which brightly illumines God's power and readiness to dispel the threat.

When Israel sets out on her way through the wilderness, the miraculous crossing of the Red Sea takes place (Ex. 13.17–14.31). One wonders if the narrative is to be regarded as a finale to Israel's stay in Egypt or a prelude to the wanderings. Probably the story serves both purposes. At any rate, Israel, preparing to move into the wastes of the Sinai Peninsula, finds herself threatened with immediate disaster. Obedience to God's call seems to lead to an impossible situation. It is this character of the story which makes it an appropriate prelude to the ensuing wanderings.

Neither the capricious mind of a reckless adventurer nor the compulsion inherent in an overpowering national misery have led Israel to face the threat of annihilation. God's command is the driving force of this precarious expedition which, from the very beginning, appears to be a march into the open gates of death. The peril which meets Moses and his people at the Red Sea is the proper exordium of many more dangers which lie ahead. But that is not all. The story is equally the heralding of God's continuous help. Yahweh's words to Israel on the eve of the theophany at Sinai are the most authentic commentary to all events during the exodus:

> You have seen what I did to the Egyptians, and how I bore you on eagles' wings and brought you to myself (Ex. 19.4).

Of all the proofs of divine succour during the exodus no single one has left such an indelible stamp on Israel's memory as the deliverance from the army of Pharaoh and the miraculous crossing of the sea.

The superabundance of water frightens Israel at the sea. Soon it is to be the lack of water which puts her into an equally precarious situation. At several points of the journey the desert provides no means to quench the thirst of the wandering people.

In the wilderness of Shur, they have no water for three days, at Marah the water is bitter so that it cannot be used (Ex. 15.22–23), and again in the wilderness of Sin no water can be found (Ex.17.1; Num. 33.14). There are other narratives which tell about the lack of food (e.g. Ex. 16.3). The way through the wilderness imposes on Israel a life full of difficulties and miseries. The most basic human needs—food and drink—are barely ensured. But whenever Israel suffers thirst, water is given (Ex. 15.25; 17.5–6); whenever there seems to be no food, sustenance is provided (Ex. 16.35). There is a remarkable detail in the story of the manna. God commands Moses to tell the people to gather only one day's portion each morning and two days' portion on the day preceding the Sabbath (Ex. 16.4–5). As usual, the Israelites do not keep this commandment; they gather more, keep it overnight and in the morning it is worm-eaten and foul (Ex. 16.20). This is characteristic of the way in which Yahweh helps his people in the wilderness—from day to day. Israel is not permitted to live in security lest she forget that she is utterly dependent on her God. She receives daily bread, and a daily portion only, from the hand of God. God's help does not miraculously change the wilderness into a paradise; the desert situation cannot be forgotten, not even for one day. The manna story in Ex. 16 closes with the remark that 'the people of Israel ate the manna forty years, till they came to a habitable land' (Ex. 16.35). Throughout their wanderings, throughout those years, Israel has to be content with the bread of the wilderness. There is a promise of better land ahead, a land flowing with milk and honey, but as long as the way through the wilderness lasts God's help has the form of daily rations of simple food.

One after the other the exodus stories are manifestations of Yahweh's help for his people. And yet it would be a gross misunderstanding were we to see in these deliverances from physical destruction the supreme examples of God's intervention for Israel. Much more happens in the wilderness than a chain of miraculous rescues from danger. Two events take place which are once and for all decisive and normative for the religious life of Israel: the revelation of God's name, and the establishment of the covenant and the giving of the law. In so far as Israel owes her national existence to the belief and the religious institutions which

Israel in the Wilderness

grew out of these events,[1] it can be said that in the wilderness Israel was born as a nation.[2]

(b) The Revelation of God's Name

The first of these crucial events is the revelation of God's name.[3] Of course, not all of our Pentateuchal sources connect the disclosure of Yahweh's name with the desert. In the P version this takes place in Egypt (Ex. 6.2). But in the JE strand of the tradition both J and E, although in different ways, have important things to say concerning the knowledge of God's name which was given in the desert. E, as is well known,[4] does not use the name יהוה until Moses' vision of God in the burning bush (Ex. 3.13 f.). The elohistic narrative in Ex. 3[5] intends to establish the link between the God of the fathers who, according to this source, had not been known to the Patriarchs by his proper name and the God who appeared to Moses under the name יהוה. The place where this occurs is the wilderness (Ex. 3.1).[6]

To J also the wilderness provides the scene for a revelation of Yahweh's name. In this source, to be sure, this cannot mean that the name Yahweh is for the first time revealed to his worshippers, since J had used the Tetragrammaton from the very beginning of his account (Gen. 2.4). But in Ex. 33 and 34, where at least

---

[1] Martin Noth (*History of Israel*, 2nd ed. of ET, 1960) has argued that the basic institution in the earliest history of Israel was the amphictyony of the twelve tribes. This amphictyony was not a political organization, i.e. not a national unit in the modern sense of the word (*ibid.*, p. 105). Rather it is a religiously oriented unity in which the worship of one God and the adherence to the covenantal law were the only common bond. To Noth, the establishment of the covenant as the basis of the amphictyony does not date back to the time of Moses. But Noth's treatment of Moses which practically robs Moses of every significant function is questionable: see the critique of John Bright, *Early Israel in Recent History Writing* (SBT, 19), 1956, pp. 85 ff.

[2] John Bright, *A History of Israel*, 1959, p. 113.

[3] It is strange that H. Wheeler Robinson in his book *Inspiration and Revelation in the Old Testament*, 1946, does not devote any discussion to the connexion of God's name with the concept of revelation in the Old Testament.

[4] E.g. Cuthbert A. Simpson in *The Interpreter's Bible* I, p. 196.

[5] The verses commonly assigned to E in Ex. 3 are: 1, 4, 6, 9–22. Cf., e.g., Robert H. Pfeiffer, *Introduction to the Old Testament*, 1941, p. 170.

[6] M. Noth (*Exodus* [ET of ATD 5], 1962, p. 32) takes the word Horeb in Ex. 3.1 to be a secondary addition to the verse which originally reported about a theophany at the mountain of God in Midian.

fractions of the Yahwistic account of the establishment of the covenant are preserved,[1] the name Yahweh is explained in a way both similar and dissimilar to Ex. 3.14 (E). While the famous explanation of the name יהוה in Ex. 3.14 is given in the form of an etymology,[2] Ex. 33.19 and 34.6 f. also introduce an interpretation of the name given by Yahweh himself. Although the passages are not identical, they have their common centre in the proclamation of God's mercy which is, to J, expressed in the name יהוה.[3] The setting of this proclamation must be observed—it is in connexion with the establishment of the Sinai covenant that the proclamation of Yahweh's name is made.

Thus three of our sources in the Pentateuch, J, E and P, preserve the memory that the revelation of God's name to Israel was connected with the time of Moses[4] and two of them, J and E, have localized the event in the desert. This event was of unfathomable importance to Israel, because to know the name of a god was to these people, as to the other Near Eastern peoples of the time, a matter of supreme consequence. The name of a god or person is not an accidental means of identification; rather it denotes the essence of a being. It is identical with his soul, and in the name the person is present.[5] Only by disclosing the knowledge of his name does Yahweh enable his people to have communication with him. It must be remembered that, in Israelite religion, God's name assumes the position which in the religious surrounding of Israel is occupied by the cult images. In these cults the visible image of a god or goddess is the centre of worship, whereas

---

[1] The literary structure of Ex. 33 and 34 is unusually complicated. Eissfeldt attributes Ex. 34.1–28 entirely to J (Otto Eissfeldt, *Einleitung in das Alte Testament*, 1934, p. 223), while Pfeiffer can only discover traces of a J story in Ex. 34.1a, 2, 4, 28 and apparently none at all in chapter 33 (Robert H. Pfeiffer, *op. cit.*, p. 146). Noth (*op. cit.*, pp. 258 and 261) regards the crucial verses Ex. 33.19 and 34.6 f. as later additions, while he thinks that most of chapter 34 and several fractions of chapter 33 contain J material (p. 243). I can see no reason for separating both 33.19 and 34.6 f. from their context and, with the majority of scholars, regard them as belonging to J material.

[2] Whether this etymology is correct or not does not concern us here. For a discussion of this point, see Th. C. Vriezen, *An Outline of Old Testament Theology*, 1958, pp. 195 and 235 f.

[3] There is a remarkable similarity in style between Ex. 3.14 and 33.19. The words 'I am who I am' (3.14) and 'I will be gracious to whom I will be gracious' (33.19) very similarly express the freedom of God.

[4] Cf. John Bright, *A History of Israel*, p. 115.

[5] Pedersen, *Israel* I–II, pp. 245 ff.

Israel in the Wilderness

to the Israelites God's name is the only tangible form in which he has established his memory (Ex. 20.24). On the knowledge of this name depends both the possibility and the validity of Israelite worship in its distinct peculiarity.[1] One can therefore say that the premises of Israel's cult are established in the desert.

(c) Covenant and Law

The other event which lays the very foundation of Israel's religion is the establishment of the covenant between Yahweh and the wandering tribes and the promulgation of the law. It is centred in the Sinai tradition and thus characterized as having occurred in the wilderness. The historical reliability of the accounts which place the establishment of the covenant in the desert period of Israel has been doubted. Recent scholarship, however, tends to support the authenticity of this tradition.[2]

The importance of the covenant can hardly be exaggerated. Gottfried Quell calls the covenant idea the most significant and fertile concept which is developed in the Old Testament[3] and Walther Eichrodt felt himself justified in making this concept the

---

[1] Gerhard von Rad, *Old Testament Theology* I, pp. 182 f.

[2] G. Quell in *TWNT* II, p. 121; Th. C. Vriezen, *An Outline of Old Testament Theology*, p. 139.

G. von Rad (*Das formgeschichtliche Problem des Hexateuchs*, 1938) has stated the thesis that the exodus tradition and the Sinai tradition were originally independent, each having their roots in two distinct cultic festivals celebrated at different centres of worship. On the basis of this thesis M. Noth has attempted to trace the development of the themes connected with these traditions (*Überlieferungsgeschichte des Pentateuchs*, 1948). The setting of the giving of covenant and law in the accounts about the desert wanderings would thus have to be regarded as secondary. But a significant critique of von Rad's and Noth's thesis has been advanced by A. Weiser (*Introduction to the Old Testament* [or *The OT: Its Formation and Development*], 1961), who maintains that the exodus and Sinai traditions 'were the original component parts of one and the same festival celebrated at the central sanctuary of the tribes' (*op. cit.*, p. 89). A. Weiser's view has recently been elaborated in a thorough discussion by his pupil W. Beyerlin (*Herkunft und Geschichte der ältesten Sinaitraditionen*, 1961). If Weiser's and Beyerlin's position should prove to be more accurate than von Rad's and Noth's, the relation of the desert wandering and the establishment of covenant and law would appear to be not only the result of a process of literary growth but the manifestation of an indissoluble unit which has 'canonical weight' (Weiser, *op. cit.*, p. 88) for the Old Testament.

[3] *TWNT* II, p. 111.

guiding principle of his treatment of Old Testament theology as a whole.[1] Although the Old Testament knows of more covenants than the one into which Israel entered at Sinai,[2] there can be no doubt that the Sinai covenant is to be regarded as the basis and the norm of all future covenants between Yahweh and his people.

The covenant defines and regulates the relationship between two partners. It is used in the Old Testament to describe contracts between man and man, and in this usage the word has the aspect of a legally valid agreement.[3] Applied to the relationship of Yahweh and Israel the covenant idea still maintains the connotation of law and order, but it is then significantly defined and limited. While a covenant between man and man is a strictly bilateral agreement, the covenant between God and his people is basically a unilateral one. God alone is the active partner in establishing the covenant.[4] Not only is he solely instrumental in initiating the covenant relationship, he is also exclusively responsible for the terms of the agreement. Israel can only accept or reject the terms offered; she has no possibility of bargaining over them. However, in so far as Israel is urged to either accept or reject the offer of the covenant with God[5] she is called to make a conscious response, and this includes the element of decision and choice, a decision and choice which is altogether dependent upon a superior choice on the part of God. This covenant is the foundation of all Old Testament religion. The Israelite understands himself as predetermined by it in his active life. His cult, but also his everyday actions, the law and the prophets alike, all presuppose the validity of the covenant with Yahweh.

In the books of the Pentateuch it is the law which is more particularly placed in the closest possible connexion to the

---

[1] Walther Eichrodt, *Theologie des Alten Testaments*, 1st ed., 1933.
[2] The Priestly Code contains two covenants before the Mosaic one: the first with all mankind instituted with Noah (Gen. 9.9 ff.), the second one made with Abraham (Gen. 17). It is certain that these pre-Mosaic covenants are the result of theological reflection rather than imprints of historical memory. Historically speaking, the Mosaic covenant is the primary one in the likeness of which older covenants were construed.
[3] Cf. e.g., Gen. 31.44 ff.; I Sam. 18.3.
[4] Th. C. Vriezen points out (*Old Testament Theology*, p. 141) that in all the sentences which connote the 'conclusion', 'foundation', and 'giving' of the covenant, Yahweh is the subject of the verb.
[5] E.g. Ex. 24.3, 7; Josh. 24.15.

Israel in the Wilderness

covenant. Yahweh, who establishes the covenant, is also the lawgiver. The question of the precise relationship between covenant and law is complicated and cannot be discussed here. It seems to be firmly established, however, that neither can the law and its fulfilment be regarded as the premise of the covenant, nor did there ever exist a covenant relationship between Yahweh and his people without some pronouncement of law.

The law—the Decalogue in its various forms as well as other sets of commandments in the Pentateuch—is not the expression of a general and universal demand of morality; rather it is to be understood as the explication of the covenant. It defines the mode of human behaviour which is or is not in keeping with the covenant relationship.[1] The commandments are part and parcel of the covenant itself. This is clearly expressed in Deut. 27.9 f., although here the technical term 'covenant' is not used:

> Hear, O Israel, this day you have become the people of the Lord your God. You shall therefore obey the voice of the Lord your God, keeping his commandments and his statutes, which I command you this day.[2]

Since the Pentateuch puts the establishment of the covenant and the giving of the law in the events of Sinai, it becomes possible to say that Israel's religious life as a partner of Yahweh begins in the wilderness. The desert is the place of God's initial and fundamental revelation to his people.

(d) The Election of Israel

It could well be argued that the election of Israel is prior to the self-disclosure of Yahweh, to the covenant, and to the law. The

---

[1] Gerhard von Rad, *Old Testament Theology* I, p. 192.

[2] The intimate correlation of covenant and law would be further strengthened if the reconstruction of G. von Rad is correct in his attempt to explain the Sinai-pericope as the cult-legend of the celebration of the renewal of the covenant. Von Rad's thesis would explain the reason why in the present textual order the pronouncement of the Decalogue (Ex. 20) precedes the establishment of the covenant (Ex. 24). This order does not indicate a theological priority of the law over the covenant, but it is the reflex of a liturgical order. G. von Rad, *Das formgeschichtliche Problem des Hexateuch*, 1938.

idea of election expresses the divine volition which works itself out on the historical plane as the revelation, the covenant, and the law. On the other hand, the doctrine of election is also the focal point in which the constituting elements of Israel's faith are all represented. It is in this sense that the election is here posited.

The primary verb expressing the act of choice on God's part is בָּחַר. It is found designating the idea of Israel's election only in relatively late material in the Old Testament, mostly and significantly, as Th. C. Vriezen has pointed out,[1] in Deuteronomy and Deutero-Isaiah. That, however, does not mean that the belief in election, in a less developed form, cannot be found prior to the composition of these books. On the contrary, the conviction that Israel is Yahweh's chosen people is much older. K. Galling has shown[2] that the Old Testament contains two, seemingly contradictory, traditions about the beginnings of Israel's election. There is, on the one hand, the account of the election of the patriarchs,[3] and, on the other hand, the tradition which sees the beginning of the election in the event of the exodus. Galling has convincingly argued that, contrary to the impression which the reader of the Old Testament gets through the sequence of the books of Genesis and Exodus, the tradition which claims the delivery from the Egyptian bondage as the root of the idea of election is the older one. The stories about the patriarchs are a 'retrojection of election'[4] into the past. While in the election of Abraham the nation which is to issue from him is already represented, it is not until the events of the exodus that Israel as a whole is declared to be the elect of Yahweh. Now, for the first time, it is announced that Israel is the son of God. This is the message which Moses has to bring to Pharaoh (Ex. 4.22 f.), and the election in the exodus is presented in Hosea (11.1) and Jeremiah (2.2) in terms of Israel's sonship. The same understanding, without the use of the son image, is stated in Deut. 32.10 and in Ezek. 20.5 f.

It is not necessary here to investigate the theological implication

---

[1] Th. C. Vriezen, *Die Erwählung Israels nach dem Alten Testament* (Abhandlungen zur Theologie des Alten und Neuen Testaments, 24), 1953.
[2] Kurt Galling, *Die Erwählungstraditionen Israels.*
[3] E.g. Gen. 12.2 f.; 26.3 f.
[4] H. Wheeler Robinson, *Inspiration and Revelation in the Old Testament*, p. 151.

Israel in the Wilderness

of the doctrine of election even in its broadest outline.[1] It must suffice to say that Israel's belief in Yahweh's choice which made her his elect people is grounded in the exodus event. Once more, the wilderness[2] is the womb of a fundamental datum of the religion of the Old Testament without which its development would be unintelligible.

(e) The Rebellion of Israel

The constitutive elements of Israel's faith and life are rooted in the wilderness tradition. And yet there is another element in this same tradition marking a glaring contrast to those salutary events —the element of the people's murmuring on the way. In the Old Testament the march in the wastes of the Sinai peninsula is never said to have originated in the Israelites' own mind, but is always reported to be initiated by God's command, mediated through Moses (e.g. Ex. 4.10). Here the fact that the people lose courage on the way is not interpreted as the breakdown of a noble decision, but as a rebellion against God. In the course of the long sojourn there is indeed much reason why Yahweh's command to leave Egypt is felt by the wanderers to be an unbearable burden. The threat of death accompanies them continually in various disguises: in the form of Pharaoh and his army (Ex. 14.10 f.), in lack of water (Ex. 15.24; 17.2) and of bread (Ex. 16.2 f.), and in the shape of giants who seemingly bar the entrance to the promised land (Num. 14.2 f.). The demand on Israel's faith, imposed by God's command, is too great; she is tired of the conditions of the desert life (Num. 21.5) and speaks out against it. The unwillingness to undergo the trials of the wilderness is depicted as disobedience to God (Num. 21.5) or, which is obviously the same thing, to Moses (Ex. 15.24; 17.2) or Moses and Aaron (Ex. 16.2; Num. 14.2).

The narrative of the golden calf is clearly the culmination of the exodus stories in this respect.[3] It is equally clear that, at least in its

[1] For this see H. H. Rowley, *The Biblical Doctrine of Election*, 1952; Th. C. Vriezen, *Die Erwählung Israels nach dem Alten Testament*.

[2] It may be remarked again that the exodus in the understanding of large portions of the Old Testament comprises as a unit the deliverance from Egypt and the wandering in the desert, cf. pp. 16 f.

[3] The literary analysis of Ex. 32 is, as so often in Exodus, a matter of

present form, the narrative cannot have been a part of the genuine desert traditions. The parallels to the events recorded in I Kings 12.28 ff. are so close, up to the point of verbal agreement, that an interrelationship of the two passages must be assumed. In I Kings 12.28 ff. we are told how Jeroboam I instituted two cultic centres at Bethel and Dan, both of which contained a golden calf, apparently intended to be an image of Yahweh. The use of images in the worship of Yahweh was no innovation (Judg. 17.1–6), and perhaps Pedersen is right when he concludes from the desire of Jeroboam I to imitate the cult in Jerusalem (I Kings 12.27) that the official worship of Yahweh in Jerusalem at this time also included the image of a bull which was only removed later on, possibly by Asa.[1] At any rate, the polemic against a Yahweh-Baal cult, expressed in the worship of the golden calves, is in Ex. 32 transposed into the setting of Sinai. The intention, however, to give the fight against Canaanite cult practices as ancient an authority as possible can only partially explain the significance of Ex. 32 in its context. More important than this is the position of the chapter between the original establishment and the renewal of the covenant (Ex. 24 and 34). The story of the golden calf stands between these events as the dark interlude which threatens to nullify the covenantal relationship of Yahweh and Israel at its very inception. The inexplicable and ineradicable bias to idolatry which assumes the shape of the worship of images when Israel is surrounded by Canaanite culture is already operative in the desert at the time of the establishment of the covenant. It is absolutely amazing to realize that the mind who placed Ex. 32 in the sequence of the Exodus stories has thereby made the confession of Israel's immediate and radical disobedience to her God. The desert is not only the scene of God's inaugural revelation, it is also the scene of Israel's sin which comes to light at once.

There are some details in the pericope of the golden calf which specially throw light on the concept of the wilderness. Neither

---

controversy. For example, Eissfeldt attributes the bulk of the chapter to the Elohist (*Einleitung*, p. 224), while Noth prefers to assume a secondary addition to J, as the connexion with I Kings 12 makes it impossible to regard Ex. 32 as an original part of the J document if the common dating of J in the era of Solomon is to be retained (*Exodus*, p. 246).

[1] Pedersen, *Israel* III–IV, p. 640.

Israel in the Wilderness

Aaron nor the Israelites as a whole mean to substitute another god who led them through the wilderness for Yahweh. Adoring the golden image they mean to celebrate a feast for Yahweh (Ex. 32.5). The image is to represent the gods 'who have brought you up out of the land of Egypt' (Ex. 32.4).[1] Israel is not conscious of forsaking Yahweh, but she wants to possess him in visible and tangible form.[2] The bull or calf, the central image of Canaanite worship of fertility, is the representation of the blessings of nature in a land of agriculture.[3] To worship of fertility deities belong public feasting and sexual orgies, a trait displayed in Ex. 32.6.[4] Plainly, the Israelites are tired of the life in the desert; they long for plentiful food and enjoyment. A land of rich fertility had been promised them, it is true, but the time is not yet ripe for them to enter it. Only God himself can rightfully bring their wanderings to an end, as he alone had led them out into the wilderness. Israel makes an attempt to shorten the time of waiting, seeking to escape the desert before God allows them to do so. The result is devastating. Not only is this shown by the punishment which befalls the people who try to abandon the desert prematurely;[5] much more important is the fact that Israel by worshipping the golden calf has practically revoked the covenant with Yahweh. Israel's life under God, hardly begun in the wilderness, is disclaimed on the spot. The revelation of the name of God is forgotten in exchange for a visible image. In consequence, both the covenant and the law are broken, which is symbolized by

---

[1] The strange plural 'gods' in Ex. 32.1 and 4 could be caused by the hidden allusion to the two images of Jeroboam I or, perhaps, by the intention of the author to depict the tendency to worship many gods even under the cover of a Yahweh cult.

[2] Noth thinks that the golden calf cannot have been meant to be a representation of Yahweh, but rather the pedestal on which he was supposed to sit, as a representation of the godhead in the figure of animals is, except for Egypt, unknown in the ancient Near East (*Exodus*, p. 247). There is no doubt, however, that in our text Yahweh is identified with the calf (Ex. 32.4).

[3] Pedersen, *Israel* III–IV, p. 509.

[4] וַיָּקֻמוּ לְצַחֵק in Ex. 32.6, rendered in RSV with 'They rose up to play', means sexual abandonment, as the parallel Gen. 26.8 shows.

[5] The passage concerning the punishment shows secondary additions. Three different punishments can be distinguished: (*a*) Moses makes the people drink the water which contains the image ground to powder (v. 20); (*b*) the Levites execute 3,000 of the trespassers (vv. 25–29); (*c*) v. 34 indicates the postponement of the punishment on the part of Yahweh.

Christ in the Wilderness

Moses smashing the tables of the law when he sees the crowd dancing around the golden image (Ex. 32.19). The election of Israel as Yahweh's chosen people is all but rendered void (Ex. 32.10). Israel, called by Yahweh in the wilderness, in her attempt to exchange the worship of her God with a godhead of nature, radically impairs the foundation to which she owes her existence. It takes a new, completely unmerited act of divine grace to restore the broken bond in the renewal of the covenant (Ex. 34).[1]

(f) Deuteronomy

It has often been observed that one of the characteristic features of the book of Deuteronomy is its parenetic character.[2] The history of the desert wanderings is widely used in the book, but the events are not reported for their own sake. In Deuteronomy the history of the sojourn is told for the lesson which can be learned from it; it serves the function of a text for a sermon.[3]

In order to understand the significance of the wilderness theme in Deuteronomy it is necessary, first of all, to realize the historical position of the book. Gerhard von Rad has said that Deuteronomy addresses Israel in an interim period, half-way between her election and the fulfilment of the promises.[4] The book, at least mainly in the form in which we have it today, was written not very long before it was found in the temple in 621 BC during Josiah's reign.[5] It is styled, however, as the last words of Moses

---

[1] As in the history of creation and fall, the disobedience of man immediately follows the divine grace. There can be no doubt, however, that in the story Ex. 32 the Israelite believer committed to memory the experience of himself as a sinner which, in the account Gen. 3, he widened to give universal validity. In the realization of his own sinfulness, the Israelite was forced to pronounce the sinfulness of mankind (cf. Karl Barth, *Kirchliche Dogmatik* IV, 1, p. 474 [ET, p. 427]). Noth may well be right in suggesting that the motif of the murmuring, which finds its powerful climax in the much later story of the golden calf, has its origin within the traditions about the wilderness (*Exodus*, p. 113). If this is so, the wilderness experience of Israel is the bud out of which developed the Christian doctrine of original sin.

[2] E.g. S. R. Driver, *Deuteronomy* (ICC), p. xix.

[3] It will not be unfair to say, however, that Deuteronomy is throughout more true to its text than the great majority of sermons to which we are so frequently exposed!

[4] Gerhard von Rad, *Old Testament Theology* I, p. 223.

[5] G. Ernest Wright ('Deuteronomy', in *The Interpreter's Bible* 2, p. 324) suggests the century between 740 and 640 BC.

given to Israel while she was still on the eastern side of the Jordan before the entering of the promised land (Deut. 1.1–5), an event which took place roughly 700 years before. Seven hundred years of disobedience are disregarded and the people of Josiah's time are again addressed as the generation in the wilderness.[1] Although the fathers were disobedient, the old covenant of the wilderness is renewed (Deut. 27.9),[2] so that Josiah's generation is given a new chance to be obedient. Thus Deuteronomy takes Israel back beyond Jordan to the original place of her calling; in the desert a new beginning can be made. On the other hand, the fulfilment of the promise in Deuteronomy is still to be expected. It consists in the quiet and peaceful possession of the land and the rest in which Israel can enjoy her heritage.[3]

Addressed as the nation which is to enjoy peacefully the possession of the land, Israel is reminded of what happened during her wilderness time. Deuteronomy obviously regards it as crucial that the period in the desert must never be forgotten. This time established a lesson which the nation must needs remember in order to attain the fruition of the promise. Again and again the people are warned—remember![4] Always when the appeal to Israel's memory is made it is done with reference to the events that happened in Egypt and during the forty years' sojourn. Very clearly three things stand out when Deuteronomy recalls to mind what has occurred in this time: the miserable and humiliating condition of Israel during the period of slavery in Egypt;[5] the unprecedented and miraculous help of Yahweh during the exodus;[6] and the stubborn rebellion of an intractable people.[7]

---

[1] G. von Rad, *op. cit.* I, p. 231.

[2] Deut. 27.9 f. probably ought to be connected with 26.16–19, providing the link between chapters 26 and 28. See S. R. Driver, *op. cit.*, pp. 297 f.

[3] Deut. 3.20; 12.9 f.; 25.19. The same idea is found in the other books of the Deuteronomic history, e.g. Josh. 1.13, 15; 21.44.

[4] Deut. 5.15; 7.18; 8.2, 18; 9.7; 15.15; 16.3, 12; 24.9, 18, 22; 25.17; 32.7.

[5] 5.15; 15.15; 16.3, 12; 24.18, 22. The oft-repeated phrase 'you shall remember that you were a slave in Egypt' is typical for Deuteronomy, so typical, in fact, that it found its way into the Deuteronomic recension of the Decalogue, where it stands in the place of the reference to creation in Ex. 21.11 (P). In the view of Deuteronomy, the Sabbath is not a day of commemoration for God's rest after the completion of creation but a commemoration of the deliverance from Egypt.

[6] Deut. 7.18; 8.2, 18.

[7] Deut. 9.7.

Christ in the Wilderness

Israel has to remain ever conscious of this threefold lesson of the wilderness time if she wishes to attain the promise made by God.

The action of Yahweh through which this lesson was achieved is expressed in Deuteronomy chiefly by the use of three verbs. Yahweh tested,[1] disciplined and humbled Israel in the wilderness. The three verbs undoubtedly convey the impression that God during this time was dealing rather severely with his elect. In fact, the Hebrew words strengthen rather than soften this impression.[2] Nevertheless, it is clear that the hardships of the desert were not inflicted on the people by a harsh taskmaster who delights in severity for its own sake. In Deut. 4.34, a sentence expressing very vividly the marvel at the unmerited grace of election, the trials[3] are put together with the signs and wonders which Yahweh wrought in defence of his people. Apparently the goal of the tests, the discipline and the humiliation is entirely positive. They are solely designed to burn into Israel's heart the secret of her election with which she stands and falls—the first requirement for a life in the strength of God's election is the understanding that the elect people are completely and continually dependent on God. This is the lesson of the hardships of the wilderness:

> He humbled you and let you hunger and fed you with manna, which you did not know, nor did your fathers know; that he might make you know that man does not live by bread alone, but that man lives by everything that proceeds out of the mouth of the Lord (Deut. 8.3).

The meaning of these famous words is not the somewhat

---

[1] G. Ernest Wright holds, in agreement with the view of von Rad, that Deuteronomy stems from circles in north Israel like Hosea and the Elohist ('Deuteronomy', *The Interpreter's Bible* 2, p. 326). As one of the many points of connexion which exist between E and Deuteronomy he mentions the use of the word נִסָּה 'to test', which is indeed frequently found in the E stratum of the Pentateuch (e.g. Ex. 15.25; Wright, *op. cit.*, p. 320). The use of נִסָּה in Deuteronomy has nevertheless a distinct colouring by its close affinity to עִנָּה 'to humble', which is used almost synonymously in Deut. 8.2, 16. This affinity occurs nowhere outside Deuteronomy.

[2] יִסַּר 'to discipline' is used in Deuteronomy to describe the punishment for defamation (22.18). עִנָּה 'to humble' in the piel is often employed to denote oppression (e.g. Ex. 1.11 f.).

[3] The rendering 'trial' in RSV corresponds to בְּמַסֹּת 'through tests'.

Israel in the Wilderness

Platonic idea that man, leading a spiritual as well as a physical life, must not neglect the higher spiritual needs of his nature.[1] Rather the words convey Israel's utter dependence on Yahweh in everything. The miracle of the manna which provided sustenance only from one day to another is regarded as an illustration for the truth which holds good for the whole of Israel's existence, be it spiritual or physical—she lives day by day through God's special care alone. The words, therefore, explain the mystery of Israel's election: it is solely through the word of God that this nation exists.

The second requirement for a right understanding of her election is the necessity for Israel to understand herself. The passages which speak of God's testing Israel[2] are usually taken to mean that Yahweh intends to find out if the people will obey or not. This is undoubtedly the meaning in Gen. 22.1 and in the wilderness passages in the material belonging to the Elohist. Certainly Deut. 8.2 'testing you to know what was in your heart' seems to point in the same direction. But the Hebrew text leaves it open who the subject of the knowing is; it could be either God or Israel herself.[3]

Now, it seems that the following verse is a commentary on 8.2. Here it is expressly said that Yahweh makes Israel know that she is to live in dependence on him. It is therefore natural to interpret 8.2 in the same way. God tests Israel so that she may find out what is in her heart. Interpreted like this the idea of testing would well fit the similar one of humbling, ideas which are tied together in 8.2 and 16. The purpose of the test is Israel's self-recognition which consists in humility. Humility, and not pride, is the proper response to Yahweh's election, as Israel is not chosen because she is bigger (Deut. 7.7) or better (Deut. 9.4) than other peoples. More than that, self-recognition in the light of election even means the recognition of sinfulness (9.7). For that reason Deuteronomy repeated the story of the golden calf in Ex. 32.[4]

[1] So Driver, *op. cit.*, pp. 107 f.
[2] Deut. 4.34; 8.2, 16. Man as subject of the testing 6.16.
[3] The subject of לָדַעַת in the Masoretic text is as uncertain as it is in the RSV.
[4] Deut. 9.6–21 follows the account of the book of Exodus more closely than usual. See the table of parallels in Driver, *op. cit.*, p. 112.

This is the threefold lesson of the wilderness, learned through trials and hardships, which Deuteronomy insists that Israel must always remember: the recognition of God who chose, guided and sustained his people in an act of free grace; the recognition of Israel's utter dependence on this continued act of grace; and Israel's self-recognition in her sinfulness.

4. THE WILDERNESS IN THE PSALMS AND PROPHETS

Johannes Pedersen has stated that for the Israelite the desert was a land of curse.[1] In view of the previous discussion of the role of the wilderness theme in the Pentateuch there appears to be very little or no justification for that statement.[2] The Pentateuch, it is true, knows of the dangers which accompany the life in the uninhabited and barren wastes.[3] But based on these texts there would seem to be no substantiation for so radical an opinion. However, in dealing with the psalms and prophets the picture changes. In the Pentateuch the desert is only a foil showing off the greatness of God's actions on the one hand and the rebellion of the people on the other. In both the psalms and prophets the picture of the desert assumes a decidedly darker tint. Moreover, mythological concepts are here associated with it which give the desert an almost personal character. It is no longer simply the designation for a definite geographical area or a certain condition of the land; it now assumes some characteristics of a being which stands in close proximity to the powers of darkness and death.

It will be helpful, before considering some pertinent passages in the psalms and prophets in particular, to give at this point a

---

[1] Pedersen, *Israel* I–II, pp. 455 f.

[2] It is significant that Pedersen takes his references almost exclusively from the prophets and hagiographa. Herein lies the weakness of his presentation. The theologically relevant themes of the wilderness as the place of the revelation of God's glory and help and the passages concerning the prophets' expectation of a new exodus through the desert are entirely disregarded by him. Of course, he wants to give a picture of Israel's culture. But it is very questionable if Israel's culture can be adequately described without taking into serious consideration the theological motives which are operative in the Old Testament.

[3] Again Deuteronomy sums up comprehensively in 8.15 the underlying concept in all wilderness stories in the Pentateuch.

brief résumé of Pedersen's discussion of the wilderness.[1] In his view, for the Israelite the inhabited and cultivated country is the land of blessing, while the desert is its exact opposite, the land of curse. In the latter there is neither seed nor fruit, water nor growth. Man cannot live there, only frightening and unwanted kinds of animals dwell in this place.[2] It is the land where man takes refuge when he is driven from the community (Job 30.3-8). Wilderness and sin are correlated; whenever sin occurs even the good land can be turned into desert (Jer. 12.4). Furthermore, the wilderness is tied to the realms of death and of the deep; together with them it makes up the three non-worlds (Ezek. 26.19-21). The element common to them all is chaos, the condition where the curse prevails.

(a) The Psalms

In the psalms references to the exodus and the sojourn in the wilderness are frequent. Since the majority of the psalms belong to a period later than the compilation of our major Pentateuch sources, the wilderness theme appears mostly in a different light.[3] This comes out in the rather curious fact that the memory of the desert is seldom utilized in such psalms which give praise to Yahweh for his mighty works in Israel's history. From traditions like Deut. 1.31 one might well expect that the wilderness time would serve as one of the primary illustrations for Yahweh's intervention for which the praises are sung. That, however, is not the case. Psalms 105, 135 and 136[4] are hymns of praise which

[1] Pedersen deals with the subject at considerable length, *Israel* I-II, pp. 453-70.

[2] In view of the importance of this point for the subsequent discussions pertaining to the New Testament, I give a list of passages where animals are said to occupy the desert: Num. 21.6-9, fiery serpents; Deut. 8.15, fiery serpents and scorpions; Isa. 34.9-15, hawk (?), porcupine, owl (?), raven, jackals, ostriches, wild beasts in general, hyena—also satyr and hag, probably demons in animal form; Jer. 9.10 f., cattle and ordinary birds are absent, but jackals dwell there (10.22); Zeph. 2.14 f., vulture (?), hedgehog, owl (?), raven (?), a lair of wild beasts in general; Ezek. 34.5, 25, wild beasts. When the wilderness is turned into a paradise no lion nor any ravenous beast shall be in it—Isa. 35.9.

[3] This is presumably to be attributed to the influence of the prophets on the psalms.

[4] The three psalms are usually dated in the post-exilic period. Some scholars would date them as late as the Persian or Greek period (C. A. Briggs, *The Book of Psalms* (ICC) II, 1907, pp. 342 and 478).

gratefully remember Yahweh's salutary deeds in the history of his people. Ps. 105 recalls God's dealings with the patriarchs (9-15), with Joseph (16-22), and with the people in Egypt (23-38). In comparison to the emphasis given to these periods the reference to the wilderness time (40 f.) is very short and almost fleeting. It is remarkable that the Sinai tradition is altogether bypassed. In Ps. 135 the desert is not mentioned at all, although v. 11 refers to incidents which occurred during this time (cf. Num. 21.21-24, 33-35). Ps. 136 gives the impression of a brief recapitulation of the history described in the Hexateuch. Here the wilderness is briefly mentioned in v. 16, but the attention given to this theme is again very limited compared with other themes which occur in the psalm (creation: vv. 5-9; Egypt: vv. 10-15). Hymns of praise, written during the post-exilic period, have not found the memory of the wilderness a suitable example of Yahweh's power. If the theme is mentioned at all, it is swiftly passed.

This by no means indicates that the wilderness theme lies outside the interest of the poets who composed the psalms. The fact is that the theme retains considerable significance. But in comparison with the stories in the Pentateuch, the emphasis has changed. What in the Pentateuch has been an important, but certainly not the all-important, factor now in the psalms assumes a central position: the element of Israel's rebellion in the desert. Consequently, in psalms of confession and contrition or in psalms containing solemn warnings our theme plays a dominant role.

Ps. 78,[1] the longest psalm concerned with a representation of Israel's history, uses the wilderness theme amply for this purpose. The psalm starts in the same way as the hymns of praise, as though it were going to proclaim God's wonders in history:

> We will not hide them from their children, but tell to the coming generation the glorious deeds of the Lord, and his might, and the wonders which he has wrought (v. 4).

---

[1] Ps. 78 was compared to Deuteronomy and to Deut. 32 especially by H. Junker and O. Eissfeldt (H. J. Kraus, *Psalmen* [BK], pp. 540 f.). Eissfeldt championed the Solomonic era as date of composition. But in view of the strong resemblance of the psalm to characteristic features of the Deuteronomistic school a date around 500 is more likely (cf. the importance of law and covenant in v. 10, the similarity of v. 34 to Judg. 2.10 ff., and the importance of the lesson derived from history).

Israel in the Wilderness

But soon it is made clear that the proper intention of the hymn is to warn the present generation not to fall into the sins of the fathers (vv. 5-8), whose stubborn wickedness is proved by their history:

> a stubborn and rebellious generation, a generation whose heart was not steadfast, whose spirit was not faithful to God (v. 8).

The proof of the fathers' wickedness was first given in the wilderness:

> How often they rebelled against him in the wilderness
> and grieved him in the desert (v. 40).

By far the longest section of the psalm is devoted to the events during the forty years' wanderings (vv. 14-41; 52-53). The JE tradition is freely applied and in many cases amplified beyond the narratives in the Pentateuch. The positive aspect of God's help in the desert is not disregarded (vv. 14-16, 23-29, 52-53), but it is only told to provide the background against which the sin of the fathers stands out. The author of the psalm does not weary of describing the fathers' sin again and again in many different words: their rebellion (vv. 17, 40, 56), their faithlessness (vv. 22, 32, 42, 57); their testing God (vv. 18, 41, 56), and their craving (vv. 18, 30). But the wrath of God meets the faithless generation and the wilderness becomes the scene of terrible punishments; many of the trespassers are slain (vv. 31, 34) and the others have to spend their years in terror (v. 33).

Ps. 106[1] presents an even gloomier portrayal. In spite of its hymnic introit (vv. 1-3), it is a psalm of contrition.[2] The confession in the opening verses sets the theme for the entire hymn:

> Both we and our fathers have sinned; we have committed iniquity, we have done wickedly (v. 6).

This time the psalmist has nothing positive to say whatsoever

---

[1] Since Ps. 106 contains indubitable references to the exile (vv. 27, 47), it must have been composed during the Babylonian captivity.

[2] B. Duhm has suggested that the psalm was composed as a liturgy of contrition for festivals of mourning and fasting among the exiled congregation as mentioned in Zech. 7.3; 8.19. See Kraus, *op. cit.*, p. 728.

with regard to those forty years. His description of the sins in the wilderness is a long uninterrupted chain of iniquities, again occupying the bulk of the psalm (vv. 13–33). There is the astonishing assertion that Israel's exile is a direct consequence of the sin committed in the desert (vv. 25–27).[1] Apparently the psalmist regards the rebellion in the wilderness as so typical that he is in a position to see all future sins committed in the land of Canaan as already present in the one great and original trespass during the wandering period. Another astonishing peculiarity of the psalm is the inclusion of Moses in the verdict of sinfulness (vv. 32–33).[2] Everyone, even the great leader of the exodus, proved to be at fault before God.

In Ps. 95[3] the generation in the wilderness is the example of sinners *par excellence*. In its brevity and concentration on a few points this idea is brought home more forcefully than in any other psalm. While the first half of the poem contains a hymnic praise of Yahweh (vv. 1–7a) the second half starts, in shrill contrast with the beginning, with a serious admonition to listen to the voice of God: 'O that today you would hearken to his voice!' (v. 7b). The contrast between the first and second half of the psalm has led earlier commentators to assume that originally independent psalms were later combined.[4] But the tendency among more recent scholars is to preserve the unity of the poem and to understand the second half as a prophetic oracle which met the congregation when, with the first half of the psalm on their lips, they entered the sanctuary.[5] The 'today' (v. 7) is understood as the moment of worship when the prophetic announcement of Yahweh's word is proclaimed to the congregation. The use of the wilderness concept in Ps. 95 is, then, very similar to the one which is employed by

---

[1] This is reminiscent of Ezek. 20.23.

[2] The fact that Moses dies outside the Promised Land has been given various interpretations in the biblical tradition. Deuteronomy finds an explanation in Moses' vicarious suffering for the people (1.37; 3.26; 4.21), but there is also the tradition of a trespass of Moses on account of which he had to die before entering Canaan (Num. 20.11–12 [P]; Deut. 32.50–52). The latter view is adopted in Psalm 106.

[3] The dating of the psalm is difficult. The dates suggested range from the late period of the Judean kings (Kraus, *op. cit.*, p. 661) to the Greek period (Briggs, *op. cit.*, p. 293).

[4] E.g. Briggs, *op. cit.*, p. 293.

[5] This is the explanation of H. Gunkel, quoted in Kraus, *op. cit.*, p. 660.

Israel in the Wilderness

Deuteronomy. In the event of the proclamation of God's word[1] the congregation is addressed as the recipient of a warning and a promise; a warning not to repeat the faithlessness of the wilderness generation and a promise to enter into the rest which was originally pledged to the fathers, but which in a true sense is obviously not yet achieved.

The significance of the wilderness as the scene of the rebellion of Israel does, however, not exhaust the usage of this theme in the psalms.[2] The exodus tradition has in several psalms been united with mythological elements, apparently originating in the Canaanite culture which Israel encountered after the conquest of the land. This amalgamation which will also be found again in some prophets has considerable bearing on our investigation. The question of the extent of Babylonian and Ugaritic influence within the Old Testament is still very controversial among Old Testament scholars, but an attempt must be made to sketch the significance of this problem in relation to a study of the wilderness theme.

In Ps. 11, a brief hymn of trust sung by an individual, we find the strophe:

On the wicked he will rain coals of fire and brimstone; a scorching wind shall be the portion of their cup (v. 6).

To the modern mind this way of divine intervention on behalf of an individual believer who is unjustly oppressed seems to be quite out of proportion. But in many psalms a similar mode of thinking can be discerned. Both the affliction of the righteous and the divine help are represented in an imagery which far surpasses the actual occasion. Apparently to the believer in the Old Testament the whole structure of order in the universe was upset whenever some injustice occurred, however limited it might have been, and to rectify the situation the world governing power of God was invoked. Thus in Ps. 11.6 we find that the afflicted

---

[1] The situation of the congregation being addressed by the proclamation of God's word would be further strengthened if Weiser's assumption is correct that a proclamation of the law followed the recital of Ps. 95 in the cult—A. Weiser, *The Psalms* (ET of ATD 15 [1959]), 1962, p. 627.

[2] Occasional references to the historical events in the wilderness which add nothing of importance to what has been said above can be found in Pss. 29.8; 66.6, 10–12; 80.8; 81.5, 7, 10; 99.7; 107.4–9.

41

Christ in the Wilderness

assures himself with his reliance on the intervening strength of Yahweh, in a phrase which clearly recalls the story of Sodom and Gomorrah (Gen. 19.24). The destruction of Sodom and Gomorrah turned a hitherto flourishing land into desert (Deut. 29.23; Jer. 49.18; 50.40) and the reference to the scorching wind also implies the notion of the deadly hot winds which change verdant pastures into arid wastes.

In Ps. 18.13 the notion of divine retribution which turns the habitation of the wicked into wilderness is an element in the description of a theophany (18.7–15). The psalm is an individual hymn of praise for deliverance.[1] Here, again, the description of the circumstances of the suffering man far surpass any concrete historical situation. He knows that he is in 'cords of death', in 'torrents of perdition', in 'cords of Sheol', in 'snares of death' (vv. 4 f.), and in 'many waters' (v. 16). This description of affliction is typical for the psalms. Death, Sheol, and the Waters are specially frequently used to describe the depth of the sufferer's predicament.[2] In the suffering of the righteous he is assailed by all the powers of destruction and perdition which surround him and threaten to devour him. Sheol is the image of the underworld, the Ur-grave,[3] and behind the use of the water stands the old Near-Eastern mythology of Tiamat. The ocean, represented in this myth by a goddess, is the representative of chaos which threatens the life and the order of the universe. From the deadly embrace of these powers the believer cries to God whose coming to the rescue is described in the theophany, vv. 7–15. In the words which picture the theophany mythological and historical elements seem to be again amalgamated. The verses have caused commentators to maintain that here Yahweh is depicted as a god of weather and earthquake. But it is equally clear that the Sinai tradition has thoroughly given colour to this picture. All the elements are part of the theophany on Sinai—the earthquake (Ex. 19.18), the smoke (Ex. 19.18), the fire (Ex. 19.18), the darkness (Ex. 19.9, 16), the brightness (Ex. 24.16), the descent of Yahweh (Ex. 19.11). Of course, it is possible that the theophany on Sinai itself is already shot through with mythological elements.

---

[1] Kraus, *op. cit.*, p. 140. There is a close parallel to Ps. 18 in II Sam. 22.
[2] E.g. Pss. 32.6; 69.2; 88.6 f.
[3] Pedersen, *Israel* I–II, p. 462.

Israel in the Wilderness

But the point is that for the psalmist Yahweh's condescension to help is described in terms which indicate the memory of the fundamental intervention for Israel in the wilderness. The mythological elements serve to underline the cosmic significance of this act which, in essence, repeats itself when an individual Israelite is in affliction and his God turns to him to help him out of his troubles.

The same amalgamation of mythological motifs and elements of the exodus tradition is found in Ps. 74.13 f.[1] The mythological fight of the god with Leviathan, the dragon of chaos, is combined with the memory of the miracle of the Red Sea. The same holds true in Ps. 77.16–20. The power of Yahweh is described in mythological language, but vv. 19 and 20 make it clear that this power, in the mind of the psalmist, finds its historical concretion in the exodus of Israel.

All this does not seem to have too much bearing on the wilderness theme. There is one psalm, however, in which a description of a theophany is given in which the mythological and historical elements are united and which also contains some references to the desert. This is Ps. 68, a psalm notoriously difficult to all interpreters.[2] An explanation of the whole psalm cannot be attempted here; only vv. 6 and 7 are important for our enquiry. It is said in v. 6 that 'the rebellious dwell in a parched land'. That may be a reference to the fate of the rebellious generation in the wilderness, but the continuation of the psalm suggests that the thought of the psalmist is not restricted to this allusion. Verses 7–10 describe the coming of Yahweh in wording which shows close resemblance to the theophany in Ps. 18. But there is something added which is not found in Ps. 18. Yahweh is said to march through the wilderness (v. 7) and to make the rain pour down in

---

[1] The RSV rendering of Ps. 74.14, 'thou didst give him as food for the creatures of the wilderness', is probably not correct. The correction of לְעָם לְצִיִּים to לְעַמְלְצֵי יָם, which is adopted by Kraus, *ibid.*, p. 513, makes better sense.

[2] The bafflement of the exegetes of this psalm is reflected in the various attempts to determine the date of composition. W. F. Albright thinks of a time as early as the tenth century BC ('A catalogue of early Hebrew Lyric Poems', *HUCA* 23.1, 1950/51). H. Gunkel dates the psalm in post-exilic times, while H. J. Kraus assumes an original core composed in the period of Saul which was twice re-edited during the times of the kings and after the exile (Kraus, *op. cit.*, pp. 471 f.).

abundance.[1] There can hardly be any doubt that v. 7 recalls Yahweh's leadership during the forty years in the wilderness, but the abundance of rain cannot be found in the desert stories of the Pentateuch. Is the miracle of the gift of water out of the rock greatly exaggerated by the use of mythological language, or do vv. 9 f. refer to the final settlement of the tribes in a land where there was an abundance of water? It is hardly possible to decide this question, but whatever the original thought of the poet of Ps. 68 was, at least it seems certain that he sees in the wilderness a condition of the land which is changed into fertile ground by Yahweh's goodness. In the light of this v. 6 assumes a more significant meaning. To dwell in the desert means, indeed, to dwell in the land of curse, in a condition which is outside the merciful power of God, who turns the wilderness into fertile land. Since in Ps. 68.7–10 the allusion to the historical exodus cannot be disputed, this psalm gives a very individual explanation of Israel's wilderness time. In the desert Israel still had to live in a condition outside the grace of God. But Yahweh's care for his people resulted in giving them water which was the material medium of his grace. Moreover, the wilderness in Ps. 68 is embedded in a tradition which explained the events of Sinai in a language permeated with mythological elements. The miracle of the Red Sea is in this tradition seen as an embodiment of Yahweh's powers over chaos. It seems, therefore, permissible to interpret the concept of the wilderness in the same categories. The wilderness is one of the powers of chaos which is defeated by Yahweh when he arises to intervene for his people. The desert tradition of Israel is thus given cosmic significance.

(b) The Prophets

Ps. 68 showed us a concept of the wilderness as the land in which God's judgment prevails. The same notion will be found in the proclamation of some of the prophets, and in Deutero-

---

[1] A. Haldar in an essay on 'The Desert in Sumero-Accadian and West-Semitic Religions' (*Uppsala Universitets Årsskrift*, 1950) attempted to explain Ps. 68 on the basis of the myth of the dying and rising god. He points out that the wilderness occupies a rather significant position in this mythology. When the god dies the verdure becomes a desert in which the enemies of the god have their dwelling-place. But when the god (Tammuz) returns to

Israel in the Wilderness

Isaiah the same combination with mythological forms of thought will appear which could be observed in some psalms. There is one decisive element, however, which the prophets have all of their own. This is their expectation of a new time which Israel will have to spend in the wilderness.

Hosea is the first who clearly expresses this expectation. He thinks highly of the desert time of his people. At this period Israel was Yahweh's young son, whom he loves (Hos. 11.1–3).[1] In Hosea's own days, however, she has turned into a disobedient and depraved people who can be likened to a woman who is unfaithful to her good husband (Hos. 2). For that reason, Yahweh threatens to 'make her like a wilderness, and set her like a parched land' (Hos. 2.3). In this threat to the 'wife' Hosea apparently does not speak any more of Israel as a people. He seems to turn to another idea which is linked with the Canaanites' belief about the earth-goddess. The land is the mother of the people and her true Lord is Yahweh. If the motherland is disgraced by the worship of Baals, Yahweh will withhold the fertility of the land (Hos. 2.12), because only he can give the blessing (Hos. 2.8) and not the idols in whom the motherland trusted to receive all her fruits (Hos. 2.5).[2]

Obviously, the desert is a condition which is brought upon the country by God's wrath. It therefore seems to be the final act of judgment when Hosea speaks of a renewed leading of Israel into the wilderness (Hos. 2.14). If Yahweh's appeal to Israel does not succeed (Hos. 2.2), if the threat to take away all blessings from the country does not prevail (Hos. 2.9–13), then there seems to be only one possibility left; Israel has to be expelled from the good country whose idols have made her stumble and placed again in the wilderness. Certainly, there is a keen note of judgment in this statement. Despite that, Hosea sees in it also the renewal of hope.

---

life, the enemies are driven back and the desert is restored to fertile land adorned with trees. While it is certainly possible that Ps. 68 is greatly influenced by Near-Eastern mythology, it seems to me impossible to disregard the rather obvious allusions to events in Israel's history. Haldar, e.g. completely bypasses the reference to Sinai in v. 7.

[1] Hos. 13.4–5 shows that the time in Egypt, to Hosea's thinking, is also the time of the desert. See also Jer. 2.2 f.
[2] Cf. H. W. Wolff, *Hosea* (BK), p. 40.

In the wilderness the old status of Israel, the status of love and trust in God, will be restored. There, Yahweh will again 'speak tenderly' to his people.[1]

Thus a return to the wilderness is also a return to the grace of God. The word return, used consistently by Hosea, is the RSV rendering of שוב translated by the Septuagint with ἐπιστρέφομαι.[2] Hans Walter Wolff has recently published a paper on the concept of שוב in the prophetic books of the Old Testament which is of

[1] It has often been suggested that the prophets', and particularly Hosea's, prediction of a renewed wilderness time of Israel can be understood as a protest of certain circles within Israel in which the ancient nomadic traditions of the tribes were still powerful against the effeminate influences of Canaanite culture which tended to dissolve the discipline and morale of Israelite life. (Following the thinking of K. Budde and E. Sellin this understanding is fully developed by John W. Flight in his article 'The Nomadic Idea and Ideal in the Old Testament', *JBL* 42 [1923], pp. 158–226. See also W. F. Albright, 'Primitivism in Ancient Western Asia', *A Documentary History of Primitivism and Related Ideas*, by A. O. Lovejoy and G. Boas, I, pp. 421–32, and Robert T. Anderson, 'The Role of the Desert in Israelite Thought', *JBR* 27.1, pp. 41–44.) A reactionary movement within Israel which held on to the old nomadic way of life did, indeed, certainly exist. Jer. 35 relates the meeting of the prophet with the Rechabites whose customs are a protest against the assimilation of Israel to Canaanite culture. They obviously preserve a nomadic way of life (Jer. 35.6 f.) and their origin seems to date back to the times of Jehu (II Kings 10.15 f.). Perhaps the Rechabite movement was an outcome of Elijah's struggle against the syncretism under Ahab. The friendly relationship between Jeremiah and the Rechabites reported in Jer. 35 is noteworthy and there can be no doubt that the Rechabites' opposition to Canaanite cult practices would have the full approval of all prophets. However, it would seem that the point is often overdone. The prophetic announcement of a second time of Israel in the desert was not primarily caused by a reaction to cultural patterns. (1) None of the prophets was, as far as we can see, a member or direct supporter of the Rechabite community. (2) The prophets see the retreat to the wilderness as a judgment of God, not as a return to an ideal cultural situation. To the Rechabites the return to the desert could not have been an outcome of Yahweh's punishment. (3) Consequently, nowhere in the prophets is the nomadic form of life as such made a requirement of God's law. It is not a standard to the prophets which could be equated with the 'pure and simple life and religion of the fathers' (Flight, *op. cit.*, p. 162), nor the 'golden age . . . when simplicity of faith in Yahweh was easy under the ideal conditions of nomadic life' (*ibid.*, p. 215).

[2] שוב is the Hebrew word underlying the New Testament conception of μετανοεῖν, although the LXX does not use μετανοεῖν as a translation of שוב. For a detailed discussion of the linguistic problems and correlations of the words mentioned, see *TWNT* IV, pp. 985–7, and John W. Bowman, *The Intention of Jesus*, 1943, pp. 29–31.

great importance for our question.[1] Wolff begins by pointing out that שׁוּב is basically an everyday word with no religious significance. It denotes some kind of turning, either turning from something (with מִן), or turning to something (with אֶל, עַל, עַד, לְ). שׁוּב can also be used in connexion with another verb and then it describes a repetition (e.g., Jer. 18.4). Combining the basic meanings of the word, turning and repetition, Wolff arrives at the conclusion that שׁוּב is most aptly translated 'return'. The observation of the linguistic characteristics of the word is strengthened by its usage in the eight-century prophets—שׁוּב, in the religious employment of the word, basically connotes a return to the original relationship with Yahweh.[2] The return to a genuine status of filial relation is nothing else but a return to the desert. Wolff attempts to show that already in Amos this idea is predominant. The forty years in the wilderness are to Amos not only a model of God's helping power (2.10), but also a time of normative character for the right kind of worship in Israel (5.25). Wolff relates these verses to the passage 4.6–11, where God grieves over Israel's refusal to return to him although he brought manifold disasters upon them. Wolff suggests, therefore, that already in Amos the motif of return is rooted in the wilderness tradition. In the book of Amos the argument can only be advanced by inference, but in Hosea the intimate correlation of the wilderness and the return is obvious: Israel has to return to Egypt, which is the same as the return to the desert (Hos. 2.14), because she has refused to return to God (Hos. 11.5). Therefore, Wolff points out, in the oldest stratum of the Old Testament prophecy, return to God is return to the beginning of God's history with his people, a return to the wilderness (p. 137). Wolff also notes that in the early prophets, including Isaiah, שׁוּב is never used in prophetic admonitions, but exclusively in proclamations of rebuke or of promises of a future action of God. That is to say, Amos, Hosea and Isaiah never call the people to return to God. They either scold them for their constant refusal to return, through which Israel has forfeited the possibility to change (e.g. Hos. 5.4), or they declare a time of renewed grace when some divine action

[1] H. W. Wolff, 'Das Thema "Umkehr" in der Alttestamentlichen Theologie', ZTK 48. Jahrgang, 1951, 2. Heft, pp. 129–48.
[2] 'Rückkehr in das ursprüngliche Jahveverhältnis', p. 134.

will liberate Israel so that it will have the possibility of returning to God (e.g. Hos. 3.4 f.). Israel, in the teaching of these prophets, does not have the choice to return to God at any time. The word שוב does not denote basically the freedom of the human will to make an ethical decision in turning to God, but it points to a certain status in which alone Israel's filial relationship to God can be renewed and which God, through his judgment, will reestablish in the future—the status of Israel in the wilderness. From Jeremiah on שוב is used increasingly in the imperative form as an admonition. But Wolff thinks that even in Jeremiah and Ezekiel 'the call to return is founded on, or at least accompanied by, the promise of salvation'.[1]

It may be that Wolff's treatment of the later stages of prophecy requires some modification, but the main argument of his paper is convincing—the root of the prophetic usage of שוב is the idea of Israel's time in the wilderness as the genuine status of Israel's sonship to God, into which Yahweh is going to lead his people again.[2]

Ezekiel, in some contrast to Hosea, in speaking of a second exodus of Israel into the desert paints a picture in which the dark colours are most clearly predominant. In Ezekiel 20, God com-

---

[1] *Ibid.*, p. 143.
[2] In Jeremiah, prophecies concerning a second sojourn of Israel in the wilderness cannot be found. Nevertheless, the prophet appears to share a concept of the wilderness very close to Hosea's. To him also, the time of Israel's original relationship to Yahweh in the desert is idealized—at this time a state of mutual love prevailed (2.2). The chapter containing the great prophecy of the new covenant begins with another reference to the wilderness (31.2), 'The people who survived the sword found grace in the wilderness, when Israel sought for rest.' The wilderness here apparently refers not to a condition of the soil but to the ruined and desolate state of the cities (A. Weiser, *Jeremiah* [ATD], 4th ed., 1960, p. 275). This is Jeremiah's usage of the word throughout his book (cf. 4.23–28; 22.6; 32.43; 33.10, 12). In 31.2, the allusion to the Sinai tradition is, on the other hand, unmistakable ('To find grace in the wilderness'—Ex. 33.12 f., 16 f. The appearance of the Lord from afar, 31.3—Ps. 68.7 f.; the 'rest' is an integral part of the wilderness tradition in Deuteronomy, cf. Deut. 12.9). That suggests that to Jeremiah the destruction of the cities of Judea amounts to a reduction of Israel to the wilderness condition. In this condition a new covenant of grace will be initiated (31.31). Perhaps it is possible to make the conjecture that Jeremiah does not expect a new exodus into the wilderness, because he sees the wilderness already present in the destruction of the land. He does not expect the infliction of Yahweh's judgment in the future; he exists already in the midst of it.

Israel in the Wilderness

mands the prophet to tell the elders of Israel of the 'abominations of their fathers' (Ezek. 20.4). The great example of the fathers' idolatry is the exodus story, which is divided by Ezekiel into three distinct periods—the time in Egypt (20.5–9), and the first (20.10–17) and second (20.18–26) generations in the wilderness. In these three periods we find the same pattern. Yahweh makes a solemn covenant with the people, the rebellion of the nation follows, and finally God wants to pour out his wrath, but for his name's sake he helps them again, thus beginning a new period of grace and immediately ensuing rebellion. The history of Israel, therefore, gives the odious impression of futile repetition. None the less, to the second generation in the wilderness Yahweh swore that in due time he would scatter them among the nations (Ezek. 20.23), and now, in Ezekiel's own days, God fulfils his oath in Israel's Babylonian captivity.[1] This time God's wrath seems to be at work ultimately, and consequently the elders of Israel despair of being singled out of other nations to be Yahweh's elect (Ezek. 20.32). At this point Ezekiel announces a new exodus into the wilderness. In the first exodus Israel was led to 'the wilderness of the land of Egypt' (Ezek. 20.36); in the second, after the scattered people are gathered (Ezek. 20.34), it will be conducted to 'the wilderness of the peoples' (Ezek. 20.35).[2] So far this sounds like a prelude to a new period of divine compassion and succour. But this time Israel is brought into the wilderness to be judged (Ezek. 20.35–38). As on Mount Sinai, she will again be confronted with God face to face, but now the purpose is not to renew the covenant, but to purge every transgressor and rebel from the nation (Ezek. 20.38). Ezek. 20 finishes on a note of hope; there will be some left after this act of purification to return to the 'land of Israel' and they shall be 'as a pleasing odour' to their God (Ezek. 20.41). But the setting of the wilderness as such to Ezekiel is the place of judgment alone—the horrors of God's punishment to the evildoers are connected with this locality. In this, Ezekiel is distinguished from Hosea, for whom the

---

[1] It is noteworthy that the phrase 'wilderness of the peoples' does not appear to convey any specific geographical location. It is formed as counterpart to 'wilderness of the land of Egypt'. Thus wilderness in Ezekiel is more a theological image than a definite location. Cf. W. Zimmerli in *Ezechiel* (BK), pp. 455–6.

[2] Cf. Ps. 106.27.

Christ in the Wilderness

epoch of Israel's renewed worship begins in the wilderness.[1]

The aspects of a fearful menace and a great hope which characterize Hosea's and Ezekiel's predictions concerning a second wilderness period for Israel are closely knit together in the preaching of Deutero-Isaiah.[2] This prophet, whose ministry takes place in the latter part of the exile period, announces Yahweh's merciful will to a despondent people. Good news for them is to be proclaimed and gladness is to be announced for a mourning people. Isa. 40 seems to open the scene with a description of the council of Yahweh.[3] A herald announces the coming of the Lord to the towns of Judah (40.9) and to Zion (52.7 f.).[4] The return of God to the desolate Jerusalem is a picturesque figure of speech which has the same meaning as other passages proclaiming the return of the exiled people to their land. Jerusalem's iniquity is pardoned, her sufferings have an end (40.2), Yahweh will jubilantly take possession again of his seat in Jerusalem and will collect his scattered people from all quarters (43.5–7) so that they can gladly return to the land of their heritage (51.11). This exodus out of the dispersion back to

---

[1] In Ezekiel's parable of the shepherds of Israel (ch. 34) there is a rather difficult reference to the wilderness. The word seems to oscillate in different shades of meaning. The sheep, symbolizing the people of Israel, are said in 34.25 to 'dwell securely in the wilderness'. This statement simply refers to the custom of Palestinian shepherds who find sufficient pasturage for their herds even in arid areas. But Ezekiel seemingly associates a more penetrating thought with the word. In 34.6 the shepherds are accused of letting the sheep be scattered 'over all the mountains and on every high hill', and v. 13 makes it plain that this scattering is a symbol for Israel's dispersion amongst the peoples. The thought of 20.35, Israel's way to the 'wilderness of the peoples', seems therefore to provide the background of v. 6. Here the wilderness is an image of judgment. But when the good shepherd 'my servant David' (34.23) comes, the wilderness will be changed into fat pasturage (34.26 ff.), where the wild beasts are banished (34.28).

[2] Isa. 34–35 are included in this review of Deut.–Isa. The connexions in literary structure and thought justify this method, whether ch. 34–35 are an original part of Deut.–Isa. (C. C. Torrey, *The Second Isaiah*, 1928), whether they are a unit composed in dependence upon Deut.–Isa. at the end of the sixth century BC (O. Eissfeldt, *Einleitung*, p. 369), or whether they are two separately written chapters which once formed an introduction to chs. 40–66 (R. B. Y. Scott, 'Isaiah', *The Interpreter's Bible* 5, p. 538).

[3] James Muilenburg, 'Isaiah', *The Interpreter's Bible* 5, p. 422.

[4] The מְבַשֵּׂר rendered by LXX ὁ εὐαγγελιζόμενος is not precisely defined. In 40.9 the figure seems to be identified with Zion and Jerusalem, while in 52.7 it appears to be an individual. J. Muilenburg, *ibid.*, pp. 423 and 611.

Israel in the Wilderness

Palestine will again be a passage through the wilderness (40.3; 48.20–21). In his characteristic style, Deutero-Isaiah describes Israel's way through the desert in powerful antithetic phrases. Everything in the nature of the desert which is troublesome for the journey of the redeemed will be transformed into a condition insuring an easy passage—mountains will be made low, valleys lifted up (40.4), the desert will turn into a pool of water, full of shady trees (35.1 f., 6 f., 41.17–20; 49.10), the roadless wilderness will yield a well-prepared path (40.3; 43.19; 49.11), and the wild beasts that inhabit the waste land will do no harm to the passing wanderers (35.9; 43.20). It is obvious that the prophet thinks of this second exodus in the likeness of the first out of Egypt. Passages such as 43.16 f. and 48.20 f. display unmistakable memories of the Exodus stories; but it is also clear that the second exodus is not simply a repetition of the first. It will surpass the leaving of Egypt in that there will be no haste, no flight in fear as before (52.12; cf. Ex. 12.39). The destination of the journey, Jerusalem, was made a desert through destruction by the Babylonians. This wilderness, however, will be changed into a paradise (51.3).

At this point it becomes noticeable that the wilderness in Deutero-Isaiah is, as in some psalms, associated with mythological language. The power of Yahweh's rebuke which dries up the sea and makes the rivers a desert (34.8–15; 50.2) is a manifestation of the strength of the creator who in his struggle against chaos at the foundation of the universe forced the sea into ordered limits. The same power which was victorious over the sea-dragon, symbolizing the forces of chaos, at the beginning of time was triumphant at the crossing of the Red Sea and will show its glory again when the exiled people pursue their way home through the wilderness (51.9 f.). The creator of heaven and earth does not delight in the waste lands; when he founded the universe 'he did not create it a chaos, he formed it to be inhabited' (45.18; cf. Gen. 1.2). But under his judgment and curse the good land is turned into the state of chaos again (Isa. 34.11).[1] Thus the desert has an affinity to the chaotic state of the world which Yahweh overcame when he created the cosmos according to his good will.

---

[1] The 'confusion' and 'chaos' of Isa. 34.11 in the RSV is the תֹהוּ וָבֹהוּ of Gen. 1.2.

Christ in the Wilderness

God's judgment turned cities and fertile lands into deserts. The wilderness to Deutero-Isaiah, however, becomes a symbol of God's judgment in a broader sense than this. Not only are the destruction of cities and the barrenness of the land the outcome of God's displeasure. There is a more horrifying aspect of God's wrath which is also symbolized by the prophet with the word 'wilderness'; it is the wilderness of the human heart which has no faith in God. The disobedient heart of the people is thirsty land and dry ground on which God will pour out his Spirit to water it and give it fertility (44.3).[1] Thus, the wilderness becomes the image of a spiritual condition and the miraculous watering of the parched land a figure of the Spirit which restores life in man. The gift of the Spirit of God is more particularly associated with the wilderness theme in Isa. 63.10–14 (cf. also Isa. 32.15; 44.3). Israel's wanderings under the leadership of Moses were a march under the guidance of the Spirit of God (63.11), and the Spirit gave the people rest (63.14; LXX ὡδήγησεν αὐτούς). As the first exodus had been a journey under the leadership of God's Spirit, it is not surprising that the prophet expects a new outpouring in the time of the second exodus.[2]

---

[1] Cf. also how the gospel to the blind, deaf, lame, and dumb is joined to the description of the turning of the desert to paradise in Isa. 35.5–7.

[2] The poems of the Servant of the Lord have no clearly recognizable contact with the wilderness concept. In so far as the Servant is commissioned 'to raise up the tribes of Jacob and to restore the preserved of Israel' (49.6), an important link to the topic of the exodus can, of course, be observed. However, the desert theme plays no part in the songs. The statement that the Servant grew up 'like a root out of dry ground' (53.2) cannot be pressed, as it is an expression typical of the highly metaphorical language of Deut.–Isa. It would seem that the 'dry ground' could most aptly be explained as Israel under Yahweh's judgment and since the wilderness is an image of this condition a connexion might exist. A definite assertion is, nevertheless, made impossible by the picturesque style of the poem.

III

THE TIME BETWEEN THE TESTAMENTS

THE expectation of a new exodus into the wilderness, cherished by some of the greatest prophets in the Old Testament, did not come true quickly. In the times following the release from the Babylonian captivity down to the period of the New Testament, the hope of a new time of grace in the desert did not die out. On the contrary, it not only retained its fascination for the Jewish mind, but flared up in the heat of eschatological expectancy.

1. PHILO OF ALEXANDRIA

In his treatise on the Decalogue, Philo raises the question why the law was given in the desert. The answers which he provides show clearly how far removed Philo is from the point of view of both the Old and the New Testaments. Four answers are given by him to his question. First of all, the desert was chosen as place for the revelation of God's laws because 'most cities are full of countless evils, both acts of impiety towards God and wrongdoing between man and man'.[1] The resentment of the cultured Jew against the empty vanity of metropolitan life comes out clearly in this argument. Philo's second answer is linked to the first. He assumes that the Israelites were contaminated by the evil inflenuces of city life in Egypt. In order to prepare them for the reception of the law, God had to provide for them some time of dissociation from the old habits so that their souls might be first purged and thus made fit receptacles for his holy will.[2] This period of dissociation from wicked habits and of gradual introduction into a state of mental preparedness for the reception of the new mode of life might be called Philo's version of the meaning

---

[1] *De Decalogo* I, 2. English translation by F. H. Colson, *Philo* (Loeb Classical Library), vol. VII, 1937.
[2] *De Decalogo* II, 10–13.

of repentance in the wilderness.[1] Thirdly, a reason of practical statesmanship is advanced.[2] Since the laws were meant to govern the Israelites when they took possession of Canaan, it was expedient to have a time of practice in which the nation should be trained in the proper application of the law so that, in the event of their entering into their state of independent nationhood, they would be able to exercise with discernment the rules which were to order their lives. The wilderness is, in this view, regarded as a training field on which skills are developed which are necessary for the establishment and administration of a sound national life. Lastly, Philo states that Israel's time in the wilderness served to point out the truth that the law which she received was of divine origin and not made by man.[3] For the miracles which occurred during the wanderings were proof that the one who was able to sustain the mere life of the people was also present in the pronouncement of the law which made possible a good life in the ordinances of God.

2. APOCALYPTIC AND PSEUDEPIGRAPHIC LITERATURE

The vast apocalyptic and pseudepigraphic literature of the Old Testament contains very little which is of importance for our theme. The description of the journeys of Enoch includes a brief account of his passing through desert areas (I Enoch 28.1; 29.1). The amazing thing is that these deserts are full of trees and vegetation, and water is gushing through them. Obviously, the prophetic announcements of the change of the wilderness into fertile and beautiful land are here reflected. The vision attests the hope that in the new age every adverse condition of the world will give way to its opposite.

Of much more interest to us is *Martyrdom of Isaiah* 2.8–12. Isaiah is said to see the lawlessness of the population of Jerusalem. This is a reason for him to withdraw from the city. He first retreats to Bethelehem, but finding there the same condition of wickedness, he withdraws further with a group of others and

---

[1] Philo accepts the Greek meaning of μετάνοια in the sense of a change of mind which involves a process of reversal in thought and way of life. Cf. J. Behm, art. μετανοέω, in *TWNT* IV, pp. 988 ff.

[2] *De Decalogo* III, 14.

[3] *De Decalogo* IV, 15–17.

settles 'on a mountain in a desert place' (2.8). He and his companions are 'clothed with garments of hair' (2.9), since they are all prophets, and their food consists of wild herbs (2.11).[1] Two years they spend there (2.12) lamenting over the sins of their people (2.10). There are several interesting traits in this account. The idea of a retreat into the wilderness is here expressed, motivated by opposition to sin and probably also by a wish for separation from the transgressions of society. This attitude is similar to the one found in the Qumran community. Secondly, the expression 'a mountain in a desert place' is indicative of the association of mountain ranges and desert country which is also found in *I Enoch* 28 f. This association is of importance with regard to Mark and will be discussed more fully later.[2]

3. THE RABBIS[3]

The prophetic expectation of a renewal of Israel's time in the wilderness can be traced in several rabbinical sayings. The idea is occasionally connected with the appearance of the Messiah[4] and the eschatological struggle with Gog and Magog is expected to take place in the wilderness.[5] The tendency to fashion the period of salvation after the pattern of the first exodus is not only discernible in the connexion with the Messianic hope; it also leads to the assumption that the great miracles during the sojourn in the desert would be repeated in the last days.

The typological principle that the Messiah, the last redeemer, would be like Moses, the first redeemer, has led to the assumption that the last days would show the characteristics of the wilderness time. The Messiah is thought to work for forty years, the manna and water miracles will be performed again and many details of

---

[1] Traditions must have existed in Israel which regarded the garment of hair as a sign of the prophet (II Kings 1.8; Zech. 13.4). The similarity to the appearance of John the Baptist is striking. Since this is the dress of the wilderness nomad (C. H. Kraeling, *John the Baptist* [1951], pp. 14 f.), does this mean that in certain groups the prophet was understood to be a man of the wilderness?

[2] See pp. 108 ff..

[3] I am dependent in this section on R. Kittel, art. ἔρημος, *TWNT* II, p. 656, and on J. Jeremias, art. Μωυσῆς, *TWNT* IV, pp. 864–7.

[4] Kittel, *art. cit.*, p. 656.

[5] *Ibid.*

Moses' life will be duplicated in the life of the Messiah.[1] The idea is so strongly attested that it could be held to have moulded the form of Jewish eschatological hope more deeply than any other.[2] The redemption from Egypt seems to have been the predominant model for the expectation of the final redemption in rabbinical thought.

4. JOSEPHUS

The great influence of the wilderness motif on the Messianic ideology is seen in its political implications in several passages in Josephus. Since the Messiah was believed to arise in the wilderness and gather the people there, the Judean desert was repeatedly the scene where Messianic movements were gathering, although the various movements apparently had different political colours. Josephus, in his description of the Jewish war being unfriendly disposed against any Jewish group which refused to collaborate with the Romans, mentions Messianic circles who under the pretence of divine inspiration caused tumult and demonic enthusiasm amongst the population.[3] This group is introduced immediately after a description of the assassinations committed by fanatical zealots,[4] and thus a close connexion between these sections of the community is indicated. The leaders of the Messianic movement lead the people out into the desert, promising them miracles from God as the first signs of their freedom. The signs of freedom (σημεῖα ἐλευθερίας) are probably to be understood as Messianic miracles, although Josephus does not say so, in particular as repetitions of the historic miracles of Israel's exodus. The movement breaks down, however, in a great slaughter as the procurator Felix intervenes with Roman armed forces.

The same fate meets a large band of people who follow the summons of a prophet from Egypt.[5] He and his group of followers

---

[1] Jeremias, *art. cit.*, pp. 864 f.

[2] This statement is the result of an unpublished dissertation of W. Wiebe (*Die Wüstenzeit als Typus der messianischen Heilszeit*), which is used widely by J. Jeremias in his article on Moses in *TWNT*. Wiebe's dissertation was inaccessible to me.

[3] *De bello Judaico* II, 258–60.

[4] *De bello Judaico* II, 254–7.

[5] *De bello Judaico* II, 261–3.

also emerge from the wilderness and march to the Mount of Olives,[1] obviously expecting to make their Messianic entry into the holy city. The incident of the Egyptian prophet has found its way into the New Testament. The apostle Paul, on the occasion of his imprisonment by the Roman garrison in Jerusalem, is mistaken as the Egyptian insurrectionist who headed 4,000 followers in the desert (Acts 21.38).[2] The report in Acts identifies the Messianic movement under the leadership of the Egyptian with the assassins, the most radical section of the zealots. This does not quite agree with Josephus, who seems to distinguish the groups as he mentions an alliance between them which came into effect later on (*De bello Judaico* II, 264).[3]

The prophet Theudas who assembles his followers at the Jordan, apparently preparing to move on into the Judean desert after the announced miraculous parting of the waters of Jordan had happened,[4] belongs in the same category of Messianic pretenders, and equally so the weaver Jonathan, who is also said to have promised signs and miracles and leads a force of men into the desert.[5]

A touching detail in Josephus's account of the destruction of Jerusalem in AD 70 becomes comprehensible on the same historic background. When the temple has gone up in flames the surviving Jews ask Titus as a last favour to be allowed to retreat with their wives and children to the desert.[6] Since it would be pointless in this situation to regard the wilderness as a fit hiding-place, the motive of the request can only be the hope that in the desert the final Messianic delivery will take place, changing utter disaster to triumph.

Thus, in all accounts of Messianic risings in Josephus's works,

[1] The Mount of Olives is also connected with the Messianic hope. From there the Messiah was supposed to enter Jerusalem. See the commentaries on Mark 11.1.

[2] The discrepancy concerning the number of followers in Josephus (30,000) and Acts (4,000) may be due to a misreading of the numeral symbol Λ 30,000 for Δ 4,000. Cf. K. Lake and J. H. Cadbury, *The Beginnings of Christianity* IV, p. 277.

[3] The remark of Haenchen (*Die Apostelgeschichte*, 12th ed., 1959, p. 551) that the Messianic groups were unarmed is at variance with Josephus, who speaks of them as δορυφόροι (*De bello Judaico* II, 262).

[4] *Antiquities* XX, 97–99.
[5] *De bello Judaico* VII, 438.
[6] *De bello Judaico* VI, 351.

the wilderness is invariably the place to which the pretenders lure their followers. It seems to have been established as a dogma that the Messiah on appearance would begin his work in the desert. Matthew 24.26 reflects the same dogma. The call to the wilderness is nothing less than synonymous with the claim of Messiahship.

5. THE COMMUNITY OF QUMRAN

Even before the discoveries of the Qumran manuscripts, there could be no doubt about the importance of the speculations concerning the wilderness in the period preceding and following the birth of Christ. The new discoveries have firmly underlined that fact. The settlement of Qumran is located at the edge of the Judean wilderness, and the choice of this location is neither coincidence nor caused by the force of exterior circumstances. The site of Qumran has been identified with what is called the City of Salt in Josh. 15.61.[1] Joshua lists six villages which together form the district of the wilderness (מִדְבָּר), indicating that the wilderness condition was regarded as so constitutive for the region that it could provide the name for a province at the time when the list of Judean places in Josh. 15 was composed.

The community which selected the site of Qumran as a fit location for its settlement regarded itself as the new Israel. The Damascus Document makes this especially clear. The word בְּרִית (covenant) is found thirty-five times in this book,[2] occurring in different combinations. The members of the community are conscious of having entered into a new covenant (CD 6.19; 20.12) while Israel as a whole has gone astray. The act of separation from the sinful majority and of entering the fold of the community is very significantly described by the word שׁוּב. The term has different shades of meaning in the texts of the Qumran order. The covenanter turns from the men of iniquity (1 QS 10.20), from all evil, wickedness, and sin (1 QS 5.1, 5.14, 6.15, 10.23).

---

[1] J. T. Milik, *Ten Years of Discovery in the Wilderness of Judaea* (SBT, 26), 1959, pp. 50 f.

[2] The counting of passages in CD is, of course, a somewhat questionable procedure, since the proper text of the book is hard to reconstruct (cf. J. T. Milik, *ibid.*, pp. 38 f.). The number stated above is given by H. H. Rowley, 'The Covenanters of Damascus and the Dead Sea Scrolls', *Bulletin of the John Rylands Library* 35 (1952), pp. 135 f.

The Time between the Testaments

When he enters the covenant he confesses, 'We have been corrupt, we have rebelled, we have sinned, we have been wicked, we and our fathers before us, in walking contrary to the ordinances of truth' (1 QS 1.24–26).[1] The turning from sin is at the same time a turning to God (CD 20.23), to the truth (1 QS 6.15), to the law of Moses (1 QS 5.8). The word 'to turn' or 'to return' is used several times as an absolute in CD. In these passages, the covenanters entitle themselves as the penitents of Israel.[2] Thus the community is, as the new Israel, an order of penitents; their retreat from the world of sinful Israel and their strict adherence to the law, as they interpret it, is regarded as an act of repentance.

In CD 6.5, the penitents of Israel are said to have gone out from the land of Judah and sojourned in the land of Damascus. It has been suggested repeatedly[3] that Damascus is not to be taken literally, rather it is a cryptic designation of Qumran itself. That would mean that the retreat of the covenanters is a withdrawal into the desert. However, the identification of Damascus and Qumran is not yet firmly secured,[4] and it would be too precarious to make too much of this point. But it is beyond doubt that the covenanters called themselves the exiles of the desert (1 QM 1.2).[5] That this is not a casual designation is made certain by the fact

---

[1] Quoted in the translation of G. Vermès in his book *Discovery in the Judean Desert*, 1956.

[2] The radicals שבי ישראל must be vocalized שָׁבֵי יִשְׂרָאֵל (penitents of Israel) and not שְׁבִי יִשְׂרָאֵל (the captivity of Israel). See R. H. Charles, *The Apocrypha and Pseudepigrapha of the Old Testament* II, 1913, p. 808. In two places, CD gives the phrase שָׁבֵי פֶּשַׁע (2.15; 20.17), but the absolute use of שבי is so well attested that it seems unnecessary to supplement it by פֶּשַׁע as is always done by Ch. Rabin in his translation (*The Zadokite Documents*, 1954).

[3] J. M. Allegro, 'Further Messianic References in Qumran Literature', *JBL* 75 (1956), pp. 174–87; A. Jaubert, 'Le Pays de Damas', *RB* 65 (1958), pp. 214–48; F. M. Cross, *The Ancient Library of Qumran and Modern Biblical Studies*, 1958, pp. 59 f.

[4] The older theory that an exodus from Qumran to Damascus took place after the earthquake in 31 BC must be given up on archaeological grounds (cf. Cross, *op. cit.*, p. 59). But J. T. Milik, while admitting the inadequacy of this theory, still calls the identification of Qumran with Damascus methodologically unsound (*op cit.*, p. 91).

[5] The passage in 1 QM 1.2 f. which mentions both the 'exiles of the desert' and the 'exiles from the desert of the peoples' is still obscure. The terms denote one and the same group if one is to identify Qumran and Damascus.

that the community motivates its withdrawal into the wilderness by a reference to Isa. 40.3, 'When these things shall come to pass in the Community of Israel, according to these rules, they shall withdraw from the city of the men of iniquity to go into the wilderness to clear the way of the Lord as it is written: In the wilderness clear the way of . . . level in the desert a highway for our God' (1 QS 8.12–16). The time for the clearing of the way in the wilderness has come (1 QS 9.19). In the community, the penitents of Israel gather and their retreat to and settlement in the desert is in accordance with the prophetic expectancy of a second wilderness period which will be the beginning of the final deliverance of God's people.

Accordingly, the historic time of Israel in the wilderness plays an important role in the religious concepts and in the structure of the community. Forty years elapse between the death of the Teacher of Righteousness, who is generally held to be the founder of the community,[1] and the extermination of all the followers of the man of lies (CD 20.13 ff.). Whoever the persons are who are thus called, the rising of the Messiah from Aaron and Israel (CD 19.35–20.1) will coincide with the final eschatological war, described in the Rule of War, in which the men of iniquity will be uprooted. The forty years are certainly a prophetic number: as Israel had to live in the desert for forty years, so the community has to undergo the time of test for forty years, living a life of repentance in the wilderness by strict adherence to the law and thus preparing the way of the Lord.[2] The communal structure of the community also displays the tendency to relive the exodus experience under Moses. The members of the new covenant are subdivided into tribes, thousands, hundreds, fifties and tens (1 QS 2.21 ff.) which correspond to the subdivision of Israel under Moses (Ex. 18.25; Deut. 1.15). They live in camps and they are mustered (CD 7.6; 10.2; 14.3; 20.26) like old Israel (e.g. Num.

Should this identification be false, two distinct groups are meant, one in the original settlement in Qumran, the other a splinter group in Damascus. In any case, both groups are equally called exiles in the desert.

[1] Cf., e.g., J. T. Milik, *op. cit.*, p. 74. Milik is certainly right, however, in expecting that the historical roots of the movement go back much beyond the time of the Teacher of Righteousness.

[2] G. Molin, *Die Söhne des Lichtes*, 1954, p. 140.

2.1–5.4).[1] The regulation for the life in the camp given in Num. 5.1–4 is duplicated in 1 QM 7.3–7. It seems likely that even inconspicuous details of the regulations set up by the community were imitations of the Mosaic order.[2]

It is not necessary for us to go into a discussion of details. The main point is established beyond doubt—the community did consciously choose a settlement in the wilderness. Neither contingency nor force caused the covenanters to make the desert their dwelling; in it is reflected the conviction of the supreme importance of the wilderness in the eschatological drama. The retreat to the desert and the act of repentance coincide. The reason for seeing in the wilderness the fit location for repentance is not a protest against more refined culture in favour of the rugged but decent life of the nomad. The reason rather appears to be a conviction about the form of the eschatological event. Being conscious of living in the last days before the arrival of the Messiah, the community had to prepare the way where, according to prophetic announcements, it had to be prepared—in the desert. This shows the great strength of the wilderness concept and its combination with the picture of eschatology.

[1] F. M. Cross, *op. cit.*, pp. 56 f.; W. R. Stegner, *The Self-understanding of the Qumran Community compared with the Self-understanding of the early Church* (unpublished dissertation, Drew University, 1960).
[2] W. R. Stegner goes far in drawing parallels between the wilderness time of Moses and of the community, possibly at times too far. He avers that the equation with the Mosaic period in the desert is the key for the self-understanding of the community (*ibid.*, p. vi).

IV

THE WILDERNESS THEME IN THE NEW TESTAMENT

IN order to evaluate the specific use of the wilderness theme in the Second Gospel, it will be necessary to investigate the significance of this theme first of all in other parts of the New Testament. Only in this way can it be determined to what extent Mark, in employing the desert motif, follows common usage in the theology of primitive Christianity, and in what lies his particular emphasis.[1] All major authors of the New Testament have used the motif, but the aim for which it is advanced varies as well as the importance which is attributed to it. In recent years, considerable attention has been given to the role of the exodus tradition in New Testament writings.[2] The second Evangelist, however, has

---

[1] The usage of the desert theme in Matthew and Luke is not included in this chapter. The question will be pursued separately below, see pp. 144 ff.

[2] Leonhard Goppelt (*Typos. Die typologische Deutung des Alten Testaments im Neuen*, 1939) has dealt with the typological usage of the exodus tradition in several parts of the New Testament, without attempting to trace systematically the significance of the theme. Pierre Bonnard ('La signification du désert, selon le Nouveau Testament', in *Hommage et Reconnaissance. Recueil de travaux publiés à l'occasion du soixantième anniversaire de Karl Barth*, 1946, pp. 9–18) undertook to point out the theological weight of the idea in the New Testament. He largely disregards, however, the considerable differences in the function of the theme in the various writers. George H. Williams (*Wilderness and Paradise in Christian Thought*, 1962) has an opening chapter tracing briefly the concept of the desert in the Bible in a book chiefly devoted to the development of the themes of paradise and wilderness in church history. John Marsh (*The Fulness of Time*, 1952) has also stressed the theological importance of the exodus theme in connexion with the understanding of time in the Bible. Werner Schmauch (*Orte der Offenbarung und der Offenbarungsort im Neuen Testament*, 1956) devoted a chapter of detailed exegetical analysis to the role of the desert in New Testament writings. In addition to these works, which take into account the New Testament as a whole, there are a number of others which deal with our theme in individual books, or parts of the New Testament. Concerning the Gospels, there is an essay by Robert W. Funk, 'The Wilderness', *JBL* 78 (1959). On Luke in particular, Jindrich Mánek, 'The New Exodus in the Books of Luke', *Novum Testamentum* vol. II, fasc. I, pp. 8–23, (1957). On John, Harald Sahlin, 'Zur Typologie des

so far not received a detailed study on the function of this theme in his Gospel.

1. PAULINE EPISTLES

The earliest occurrence of the wilderness tradition in the New Testament is found in I Cor. 10.1-13.[1] The generation under Moses is said to be a warning to the Corinthian congregation[2] which was written down for the sake of instruction to Christians (v. 11). The word rendered in RSV by 'warning' does not mean that the Israelites are prototypes of the Corinthians;[3] the analogy which exists between them is not one of people but rather an analogy of the situation in which they find themselves. Both the wilderness generation and the Corinthians are the recipients of divine grace (vv. 1-4). The condition of grace, however, does not provide absolute security; it can be destroyed by man's sin. At this point the analogy comes to an end. While the majority of Israelites in the wilderness fell from grace, displeased God, and were consequently destroyed (v. 5), the Corinthians are as yet only in danger of falling. They can still be warned (v. 6).

The passage I Cor. 10.1-13 is part of a long section in which Paul warns against the distortion of Christian freedom.[4] In the congregation in Corinth, there were libertines who established

---

Johannesevangeliums', *Uppsala Universitets Årsskrift*, (1950), and Robert H. Smith, 'Exodus Typology in the Fourth Gospel', *JBL* 81 (1962), pp. 329-42. William Manson (*The Epistle to the Hebrews*, 1951) has laid particular stress on the importance of the wilderness theme in the epistle to the Hebrews, although his book is written to further the understanding of the epistle as a whole.

[1] Here and throughout this chapter no attempt is made to give a detailed exegesis of the passages under consideration. The relevance of the wilderness theme is the sole object of investigation and the texts are interpreted only in reference to this aim.

[2] The RSV translation 'warning' for τύπος is in this passage correct, although τύπος has broader connotations. The word τύπος used in a comparison between the Old Testament and persons or conditions of the New Testament era includes not only the element of analogy but also that of superiority. See L. Goppelt, *Typos*.

[3] A. Robertson and A. Plummer, *The First Epistle of St Paul to the Corinthians* (ICC), 2nd ed., 1914, p. 203.

[4] C. T. Craig ('I Corinthians', *The Interpreter's Bible* 10, p. 12) titles the section 8.1-11.1 'Christian freedom'. A. Schlatter (*Paulus der Bote Jesu*, 1934, p. 7) groups together 5.1-11.34 under the heading 'The limits of Christian freedom'.

Christ in the Wilderness

the maxim, 'all things are lawful' (I Cor. 6.12; 10.23), and who were sure that they were standing without danger of a fall (I Cor. 10.12).[1] Our passage suggests that a high estimation of baptism and the eucharist was misconstrued by this group as an argument for absolute security. Apparently, the elements of the eucharist were regarded as supernatural food and supernatural drink (vv. 3 f.),[2] which might have been conceived to be a means of deification for the person who partook of it, in analogy to certain tenets in the mystery religions.[3] Against the lofty pride of this group Paul advances the warning of the rise and fall of the Mosaic generation.

Paul pictures God's gracious acts in the desert as analogous to the Christian sacraments. Israel's passing through the Red Sea is a baptism into Moses (v. 2) as the Christian baptism is a baptism into Christ (Rom. 6.3; Gal. 3.27).[4] The feeding of Israel with manna and water was spiritual food and drink (vv. 3 f.), as the Christians' spiritual food and drink is the bread and wine of the Eucharist. It is remarkable how much Paul elevates Moses to the position of a man who bears the mark of a saviour. The obvious analogy between the baptism into Moses and into Christ seems, at first sight, to place Moses and Christ on the same plane. However, this is not Paul's intention. The identification of Christ with the rock which, according to rabbinical exegesis here adopted by Paul, followed the Israelites during their wanderings[5] shows

---

[1] The problem is still controversial regarding the origins and the character of the group which opposed Paul in Corinth. While the old explanation as Judaists, originating from Ferd. Chr. Baur, is largely abandoned, the suggestions of Wilhelm Lütgert (*Freiheitspredigt und Schwarmgeister in Korinth*, 1908) and Adolf Schlatter (*op. cit.*) are still worth consideration. They regard Paul's enemies as exponents of libertine spiritualism. The latest attempt to understand the group as agents of pre-Christian gnosticism (Walter Schmithals, *Die Gnosis in Korinth*, 1956) must, however, be taken seriously. The problem has but little bearing for our purpose.

[2] L. Goppelt, art. πόμα, *TWNT* VI, p. 146.

[3] Cf. R. Bultmann, *Primitive Christianity in its Contemporary Setting*, 1956, p. 158.

[4] The idea of baptism as a process of submersion in water is achieved by Paul in the case of the crossing of the Red Sea by the simultaneous reference to the cloud and the sea. The cloud is of watery substance and so Israel is veritably surrounded by water.

[5] The legend of the wandering rock, perhaps caused by the divergent statements concerning locality in the parallel accounts of Ex. 17 and Num. 20, is partly quoted by O. Cullmann, art. πέτρα, *TWNT* VI, p. 96.

clearly the superiority of Christ over Moses. Of course, Christ is not to be identified with the rock. What Paul means to convey is the thought that the pre-existent Christ[1] was the giver of food and drink. He followed his people in the course of their journey as the water-giving rock was continually with them. This makes it clear that the position and deed of Moses are completely subordinate to the saving presence of Christ, who acts in and through the action of Moses. Nevertheless, the fact remains that in the history of the exodus Paul saw a form of the saving presence of Christ. The apostle has frequently in his letters exemplified the meaning of the Christian faith by a reference to Old Testament passages. But in no other passage which has been preserved for us has he expressly identified God's saving power in the Old Testament with the presence of Christ amidst the people of the old covenant. Is this coincidence, or does it show an extraordinary evaluation of the exodus events in the thinking of Paul? It seems to be impossible to decide this question one way or the other. At least so much, however, is certain—Paul regards the history of the wilderness wanderings as a time of God's special presence which is analogous to the condition of the Christian life to the extent that it can be used as a foreshadowing of the grace enjoyed by the congregations of the new covenant.

All Israelites were in possession of divine aid,[2] yet most of them incurred the displeasure of God (v. 5). The wilderness was the scene of singular grace, but it becomes a huge and terrifying grave; it is strewn with dead. The Israelites had all partaken of spiritual food and drink, but they ate and drank judgment upon themselves as the Christian brings judgment upon himself if he does not properly use the gift of communion (I Cor. 11.29). Thus the place of God's saving help is turned into a place of disaster. Paul goes on to greater detail, mentioning a number of specific incidents. He probably selects events which were capable of immediate application to the situation in Corinth.[3]

The first sin of the Israelites was their desiring evil (ἐπιθυμεῖν v. 6) and this is also the basic temptation of the Corinthians. Probably Paul in mentioning ἐπιθυμία does not think of any

---

[1] Cf. Robertson and Plummer, *op. cit.*, pp. 201 f.
[2] πάντες is greatly stressed four times in vv. 1–4.
[3] This is the thought of A. Schlatter, *op. cit.*, p. 291.

Christ in the Wilderness

particular form of sin or disorder which he found in Corinth. Ἐπιθυμία to him is not an exterior and concrete manifestation of sin but rather the essence of sin as the comprehensive description of man's sinful nature, of his life determined by the flesh (Gal. 5.17). Thus the nature of God's holy law can be summed up in the commandment οὐκ ἐπιθυμήσεις (Rom. 7.7). However, in continuing the theme, Paul does appear to be warning against actual forms of sinful behaviour as they occurred in Corinth. The reference to the idol worship of the golden calf (v. 7) is related to the problem of participation in heathen cults (I Cor. 10.14–22); the mentioning of the licentiousness which resulted from the idol worship (v. 8) has its bearing on Corinthian affairs, as some group in the congregation apparently regarded Christian freedom as a freedom for fornication (I Cor. 6.12–20); the admonition not to tempt God as the Israelites had done in the wilderness (v. 9) seems to point also to the issue of participation in Greek cults, as at the end of the passage devoted to this matter, Paul puts the rhetorical question, 'Shall we provoke the Lord to jealousy?' (I Cor. 10.22); also, the allusion to the murmuring of the people in the desert can be understood in the light of the possibility 'that the Apostle is warning those who might be disposed to murmur against him for his punishment of the incestuous person, and for his severe rebukes in this letter'.[1] In any case, the Corinthians are warned not to feel secure in the possession of spiritual gifts; the Israelites in the desert possessed them, too, and yet, because of their disobedience, they were destroyed.

What, then, is the function of the wilderness theme in I Cor. 10.1–13? With reference to this passage, P. Bonnard has said that the situation of the Church is not essentially different from the situation of Israel in the desert. 'Dans ce sens, l'Église du Christ est aussi "dans le désert".'[2] In contrast to that statement, W. Schmauch has maintained that neither in this passage nor, indeed, anywhere else in the New Testament are the congregations said to exist in the desert, not even in parabolic form.[3] Schmauch is

---

[1] Robertson and Plummer, *op. cit.*, p. 206.

[2] Pierre Bonnard, 'La signification du désert, selon le Nouveau Testament', p. 17.

[3] Werner Schmauch, *Orte der Offenbarung und der Offenbarungsort im Neuen Testament*, p. 34. He maintains (p. 33) that in I Cor. 10.1–13, the phrase 'in the desert' is not connected with the warnings, but solely with the punishment of

The Wilderness Theme in the New Testament

right in so far as the wilderness as a location is not the point of the analogy in I Cor. 10.1-13. The parallel between the situation during the exodus and in Corinth lies in the fact that saving grace is imparted which can be forfeited. The reference to the wilderness explains for Paul the nature of grace in general. Whenever man is the recipient of God's favour, he is freed from bondage; but this freedom never grants him the wantonness of spiritual pride and security. This rule applies whenever grace is given. It is, therefore, not at all restricted to the particular period of history during which Israel or anybody else is in the wilderness. On the other hand, what is true of the nature of grace in general has found in Israel's wilderness time a particularly striking illumination. We have seen in Chapter II how the desert tradition in the Pentateuch depicts the wilderness as the scene of revelation and murmuring. Here the inexplicable mystery of God's grace and man's disobedience are particularly close together and here this mystery is repeated over and over again. Thus it is by no means arbitrary that Paul chose this example as a warning to the Corinthian congregation. The Christian Church lives under grace, but not beyond temptation (I Cor. 10.13). 'The end of the ages has come' (I Cor. 10.11),[1] but the new age itself has not yet arrived. The believer, indeed, lives between the times. In Christ, the new age is already a reality (II Cor. 5.17) which can be appropriated in faith, but the old age is still the condition in which the believer lives (I Cor. 7.31). The wilderness is a parable of this condition. As Israel was delivered from Egypt and had to pass through the desert in order to reach the promised land, so the Christian is delivered by Christ from the bondage of the old age and is on the

---

God (v. 5), so that 'in the desert' does not denote the situation of temptation, but is restricted to the singular event of the penalty. This explanation is very forced, since all warnings given in vv. 6-10 are taken from the history of the desert wanderings. Schmauch seems to be right in denying any more than geographical significance of the word 'desert' in II Cor. 11.26 (*ibid.*, p. 34), against Bonnard, who sees in this verse a reference to the sufferings of Israel, particularly Jeremiah's (*ibid.*, p. 11).

[1] καταντάω can mean that something comes to meet man (O. Michel, art. καταντάω, *TWNT* III, p. 627). The old age (αἰὼν οὗτος) is in Paul clearly a parallel expression to κόσμος (R. Bultmann, *Theology of the New Testament* I, 1952, p. 256). Since the κόσμος is evidently still a reality with which the Christian has to reckon (I Cor. 7.31), I Cor. 10.11 does not express the idea that the new age is already the only reality of life.

way to the new age which in faith is already present.¹ But to be on the way means to be subject to trial. Pride and security are, therefore, totally out of place.²

2. ACTS

Stephen's speech (Acts 7) refers to the wilderness repeatedly.³ The exegesis of the chapter is beset with difficulties. The speech stands out, both in form and content, from all other speeches in Acts⁴ and the purpose of the discourse in the setting of Acts is hard to discover. According to 6.13 f. and 7.1, one expects an apology on the part of Stephen. However, the speech does not bear the mark of an apology at all. For that reason, some scholars have regarded it as an interpolation altogether,⁵ while others have assumed an original core which was later expanded by additions.⁶ Moreover, it is difficult to state precisely the theme of the speech.⁷ Some observations by Ernst Haenchen and Marcel Simon give us the clues for the following treatment. Haenchen gives the following reason for Luke's adoption of a long summary of Israel's history at this point. The third Evangelist wanted to show that Stephen, as the first martyr of the Church, stands in the line of a history in which patriarchs and prophets had to suffer.⁸ Stephen's speech is a résumé of the history of Israel in which the suffering of its heroes is the guiding principle. M. Simon has pointed out that the tradition on which Luke draws in Acts 7 emanated from circles of the Jewish diaspora who claimed that the Jew in the dispersion had a purer and more legitimate under-

---

¹ The same interpretation is given by C. T. Craig, *op. cit.*, p. 107.
² In II Cor. 3.4–18, Paul deals with Moses' reception of the law and the glory of his service compared to the glory of the service of the new covenant. The passage has, however, no direct importance for our theme.
³ In Acts 13.17–25 we have another, much briefer, summary of Israel's history in which the wilderness is mentioned. There is, however, no particular emphasis on the exodus tradition discernible in this passage.
⁴ Cf., e.g., Marcel Simon, 'Saint Stephen and the Jerusalem Temple', *JEH* II, 2 (1951), p. 127.
⁵ So for example F. J. Foakes Jackson. See C. S. C. Williams, *The Acts of the Apostles*, 1957, p. 100.
⁶ Several attempts are outlined by Ernst Haenchen, *Die Apostelgeschichte*, 1959, p. 238.
⁷ *Ibid.*, pp. 238 ff.
⁸ *Ibid.*, pp. 240 f.

standing of the Old Testament than the Palestinian Jewry, especially in matters pertaining to the temple and the sacrificial cult.[1]

These two motifs, the suffering of the saints and the legitimacy of dispersion, seem to be outstanding in Acts 7. Both motifs are related to each other, but it will be an aid to clarity if we deal with them separately. The theme of suffering starts with Joseph—he suffers as a result of the jealousy of his brothers and is afflicted in Egypt (vv. 9 f.). Hereafter, the generation subjugated by the Egyptians is enslaved and ill treated by its oppressors (v. 19), according to the announcement which had previously been given to Abraham (v. 6). This is the time when Moses ascends to leadership, and in summarizing the events of his life Stephen's speech obviously depicts him as the one who is rejected. Moses is not only exposed in his boyhood (v. 21) in consequence of the hostile decree of Pharaoh, he also suffers from his own fellow countrymen. When he intervenes on behalf of his brethren he is misunderstood by them (v. 25). The result of the misunderstanding is that Moses is denied by his kinsmen the office of ruler and judge (v. 27), which was indeed the office given to him by God (v. 35). Even after the performance of mighty deeds in Egypt, at the Red Sea, and in the wilderness[2] the opposition against him does not cease; the people refuse to obey him and thrust him aside, frustrating his work by the idolatry of the golden calf (vv. 39–41). What is shown in Joseph and much more forcefully in Moses is summed up and applied to Stephen's generation in the vehement indictment at the end of the speech.

> 'You stiff-necked people, uncircumcised in heart and ears, you always resist the Holy Spirit. As your fathers did, so do you. Which of the prophets did not your father persecute? And they killed those who announced beforehand the coming of the Righteous One, whom you have now betrayed and murdered, you who received the law as delivered by angels and did not keep it' (Acts 7.51–53).

[1] Simon, *art. cit.*, pp. 139 f.
[2] There is a statement in the Assumption of Moses 3.11, that Moses 'suffered many things in Egypt and in the Red Sea and in the desert forty years' (Williams, *op. cit.*, p. 108). The statement is so curiously similar in style to Acts 7.36 that one wonders if we have to hear the overtone of suffering even in this verse, although it is not clearly expressed.

The story of Israel is a story of rebellion against her helpers who were sent to her by God, and it culminated in the death of Jesus (v. 52),[1] but it is also being continued in the impending death of Stephen, who stands in the long line of succession of sufferers.

The other theme is the vindication of the divine right of the dispersion.[2] Again and again in Stephen's speech it is pointed out that God's command led his people away from their homeland to live as aliens. This aspect of the story opens, naturally, with Abraham, who had to leave his land and go abroad (v. 3). It is emphasized strongly that in the land which the audience now possesses (v. 4), the patriarch did not own as much as a foot's length of land (v. 5). It shows that any claim derived from Palestinian tradition as such is without ground, as Abraham himself was an alien in Palestine. Joseph, the next great helper of his people, also has to live in Egypt, away from the promised land (v. 9). It is here, in Egypt, that the Palestinians, Jacob and his sons, are saved from perdition (vv. 14 f.). Again, Moses at the beginning of his career had to become an exile (v. 29). He is said to have lived in the wilderness of Mount Sinai when he had the vision of the burning bush (v. 30). It is clearly with great emphasis that the speech reports, 'This land is holy ground' (v. 33). More-

---

[1] It has often been stated that Jesus is not mentioned in the speech (e.g. G. H. C. Macgregor, 'The Acts of the Apostles', *The Interpreter's Bible* 11, p. 92). The insistence of R. P. C. Hanson (*Theology* 50 [1947], pp. 142–5) is well grounded that Christ is preached indirectly through his types in the Old Testament, especially Joseph and Moses. His interpretation, however, widely accepted by C. S. C. Williams in his commentary on Acts, seems to go too far in the attempt to establish typological links between the stories of Joseph and Moses and the history of Christ. The topic of Acts 7 is not Christological in a general sense.

[2] W. Manson (*The Epistle to the Hebrews*, 1951, pp. 33 ff.) has attempted to explain Stephen's speech as a witness of the eschatological orientation of the primitive Church and the resultant world mission. The patriarchs are depicted as itinerants and seekers of the land of promise and the temple is attacked as a permanent institution because of 'the ever-onward call of God to His people' (p. 35). There is much valuable insight in Manson's position, but it seems that M. Simon, in his essay quoted above, has given a more compelling analysis of the background of the speech. It is noteworthy, however, that the eschatological and missionary orientation, stressed by Manson, are also part of the thinking of the Judaism in the diaspora which Simon argues to be the background of Acts 7 (see Hans Joachim Schoeps, *Theologie und Geschichte des Judenchristentums*, 1949, pp. 239 f.).

over, in Egypt, at the Red Sea, and in the wilderness, Moses performs wonders and signs[1] and in the wilderness he was given the law (v. 38). Thus the decisive events all happened outside Palestine during the periods of dispersion. It is significant how hurriedly the speech passes over the period from the conquest under Joshua to the time of David. All that matters is that in Palestine with the establishment of the temple by Solomon a tradition finally won the upper hand which deviated from the normative pattern given in the wilderness. Israel, as a result of her idolatry, instead of following the living oracles of God (v. 38), was given over by God to worship the stars (v. 42), and the tent of witness (v. 44) was exchanged for the temple which Solomon built (v. 47).[2] Hence, the Palestinian cult which is centred in the temple in Jerusalem is said to be a direct prolongation of the idolatry of the golden calf. The true tradition of Judaism has from ancient times been founded and preserved by Jews of the dispersion and the exponents of the Palestinian tradition are the children of idolaters who have never done anything else but persecute the bearers of the truth.

What is the function of the wilderness theme in this context? Apparently, the role of the desert in Acts 7 has to be seen in the light of a Judaism of the diaspora which was highly critical of certain elements of the cult which were incorporated in the temple worship.[3] Throughout the speech, the Israelite fathers who had to live away from Palestine are praised. Egypt and the wilderness are mainly the places which are mentioned to illuminate this intention. The geographical character of both Egypt and the wilderness is quite clear; in fact, the argument depends upon it. Perhaps the wilderness is a little more highly exalted than Egypt as the place of the sojourning fathers in Act 7. It is holy ground (v. 33). In the wilderness alone the angel communicates

[1] The expression 'wonders and signs' recalls the summary of Jesus' activity (Acts 2.22) which has its continuation in the wonders and signs of the apostles (Acts 2.43; 5.12; 14.3; 15.12).

[2] The rendering of RSV of 7.46, 'a habitation for the God of Jacob', which is based on a text not supported by our best manuscripts, is, nevertheless, to be preferred. See M. Simon, *art. cit.*, pp. 128 f.; E. Haenchen, *op. cit.*, p. 236.

[3] Hans Joachim Schoeps has pointed out that in groups of the Jewish diaspora there existed a strong criticism of both the sacrificial system and the temple in Jerusalem (*op. cit.*, pp. 220–42).

twice with Moses—once in the burning bush (v. 30), and afterward in the giving of the law (v. 38). The pattern of the proper dwelling-place for God, the tent of witness, was seen here (v. 44). It is possible, however, that the accentuated position of the wilderness in Stephen's speech is due more to the strength of the Old Testament tradition than to a conscious emphasis on the part of the author of the speech.[1]

3. HEBREWS

The epistle to the Hebrews contains a passage displaying remarkable similarities to Paul's usage of the wilderness tradition in I Cor. 10. The author of Hebrews, like Paul, is apparently writing to Christians in a situation of crisis, although the crisis is different from the one in Corinth. Hebrews is addressed to Christians who are in danger of apostasy (6.4–6).[2] Although we do not know precisely into what kind of disbelief the addressees are on the verge of lapsing, the cause of their impending lapse is expressly stated: it is the weariness and sluggishness of Christians to whom the faith has become a matter of unconcern (2.1–3).[3] To this crisis, the author of Hebrews applies the lesson of Israel's disastrous disbelief in the wilderness (3.7–4. 13). This fairly long exposition is given in the form of a quotation from the Old Testament and a subsequent explanation of it.[4] The second part of

---

[1] The position of scholars concerning the authorship of Acts 7 is as varied as the interpretation of the speech. H. J. Schoeps (*op. cit.*, p. 441) denies altogether that Stephen is an historical person while others are willing to attribute the tradition which Luke apparently used at least in part to a speech which Stephen delivered on the occasion of his trial. The position of M. Dibelius with regard to the speeches in Acts in general still seems to be the soundest (*Studies in the Acts of the Apostles*, transl. by M. Ling, 1956).

[2] It is clear that the crisis to which the letter is addressed is the danger of relapse. The classical theory which explained this as a relapse into Judaism has been revived in modified form, e.g. by William Manson, *The Epistle to the Hebrews*, 1951, pp. 17 ff., and J. Daniélou, *The Dead Sea Scrolls and Primitive Christianity*, 1958. Others prefer to assume a relapse into general indifference, e.g. James Moffatt, *The Epistle to the Hebrews* (ICC), 1924, p. xvi, and Otto Michel, *Der Brief un die Hebräer*, 1949, p. 15.

[3] A. C. Purdy, 'The Epistle to the Hebrews', *The Interpreter's Bible* 11, p. 591; O. Michel, *op. cit.*, p. 15.

[4] O. Michel, *ibid.*, p. 101, distinguishes between a predominantly warning type of exhortation in 3.12–19 and one with more stress on promises in 4.1–13. He does not, however, doubt the unity of the section.

The Wilderness Theme in the New Testament

Psalm 95 provides the basis of the argument of Heb. 3.7–11:

> Today, when you hear his voice,
> do not harden your hearts as in the rebellion,
> on the day of testing (πειρασμός) in the wilderness,
> where your fathers put me to the test
> and saw my works for forty years.
> Therefore I was provoked with that generation;
> and said, 'They always go astray in their hearts;
> they have not known my ways.'
> As I swore in my wrath,
> 'They shall never enter my rest' (κατάπαυσις).

The application given to the passage from Ps. 95 shows at once a similarity to and a difference from the manner in which Paul employs the wilderness tradition in I Cor. 10. In both letters, the writers face critical situations in the congregations and, although the crises are of a different nature, the authors refer to Israel's fate in the desert as a means of warning. But there are more specific points of similarity. Both letters point out that the Christians, as well as the Israelites, have been recipients of God's grace (I Cor. 10.2–4; Heb. 4.2); the fact that all Israelites were involved in one common destiny is stressed by both (πάντες repeatedly in I Cor. 10.2–4; πάντες also Heb. 3.16); Paul's phrase 'they were overthrown in the wilderness' (I Cor. 10.5), a quotation from Num. 14, is reflected in an equally descriptive clause 'whose bodies fell in the wilderness' (Heb. 3.17), also a quotation from Num. 14. Paul had called the wilderness generation a warning (τύπος) to the Christians (I Cor. 10.6, 11); Hebrews characterizes the relation of the former to the latter as an example (ὑπόδειγμα, Heb. 4.11).

While there are analogies between I Cor. 10.1–13 and Heb. 3.7–4, 13, Hebrews has its distinct character. The treatment of the wilderness tradition in Hebrews is governed by two characteristic expressions, both of which are borrowed from Ps. 95: the 'rest' and the 'today'. The wilderness generation was promised rest (κατάπαυσις), a promise which in parts of the Old Testament is considered as fulfilled when Israel took possession of Canaan (e.g. Josh. 1.13).[1] Hebrews, on the other hand, cannot regard this as a true fulfilment of God's promise. David, the alleged author of Ps. 95, proves this in the opinion of the writer of our Epistle, by

---
[1] See p. 33.

Christ in the Wilderness

pronouncing a new chance, a repeated 'today', for an entering into rest. This rest will be like the sabbath rest of God, a final tranquillity which will be the end of all striving (Heb. 4.3–11).[1] It is not important in the present context to decide whether Hebrews' idea of rest is derived more from gnostic analogies[2] or from Jewish sources. It is, in any case, a term denoting the eternal hope of the Christians who on this earth have no lasting city, but seek the city which is to come (Heb. 13.14). They are strangers and exiles in this present aeon wandering to their true homeland (Heb. 11.13–16). The goal of their wanderings is nothing short of the world to come (οἰκουμένη μέλλουσα, Heb. 2.5). They are indeed the 'wandering people of God' (E. Käsemann), wayfarers to eternal rest.

In Heb. 3.7–4. 13, as in I Cor. 10.13, the wilderness is of no importance as a location. Yet there exists, in the opinion of the author, an analogy between the exodus generation and the congregation to which the epistle is addressed. Israel had received a divine promise (4.2) in the strength of which she had left Egypt (3.16). Of course, the promise of rest was a real one to her, but it was frustrated by Israel's falling away from God (3.12), her rebellion (3.16), her unbelief (3.19). Thus Israel, all Israel (3.16), did not achieve the goal set for her by God's promise. The Christian congregation is, equally, a nation of wanderers to the celestial rest. The divine promise remains (4.1), but the danger of its defeat by unbelief is as real as it was to the wilderness generation. Israel in the desert thus serves, as in I Cor. 10, as a type of the recipients of grace who lost the benefit of God's favour. Both Paul and the author of Hebrews use the epic of the forty years in a way similar to Deuteronomy. The history of the exodus is a warning example from which a lesson must be drawn, the lesson being that the gift of grace does not assure the achievement of the divine purpose for which grace is bestowed; grace can be disregarded and rendered void by the disobedience of man.

[1] The idea of rest had in rabbinical explanations assumed eschatological significance. The rest of God is a metaphor of the age to come (O. Michel, *ibid.* pp. 102 ff.). Equally the sabbath had come to have eschatological meaning, notably in apocalyptic and gnostic circles (E. Lohse, art. σαββατισμός, *TWNT* VII, p. 35). Thus the combination of the rest of Ps. 95 and the sabbath is quite natural. Both concepts signify the celestial goal of the believer.

[2] This is the opinion of E. Käsemann, *Das wandernde Gottesvolk*, 3rd ed., Göttingen, 1959.

The Wilderness Theme in the New Testament

4. THE FOURTH GOSPEL

In the Gospel of John the wilderness motif plays only a very insignificant role.[1] In 11.54 a withdrawal of Jesus to some country 'near the wilderness' is reported. The verse seems to contain no more than an accidental reference to a location visited by Jesus and his disciples; it has, therefore, no further significance.

Two other verses refer to incidents from the Old Testament exodus tradition. In 3.14 the Johannine Christ says of himself,

'As Moses lifted up the serpent in the wilderness, so must the Son of man be lifted up, that whoever believes in him may have eternal life.'

The first part of the verse recalls the episode of the bronze serpent, reported in Num. 21.4–9. The point of the comparison between the serpent in the wilderness and the Son of Man is their being lifted up. The phrase 'to lift up' is one of those oscillating expressions of the fourth Evangelist embracing a profound paradox. It signifies both the going of Jesus to the Father (7.33, 14.2) and his crucifixion (12.33).[2] The incomparable exaltation of the one who descended from heaven (3.13) to the realm of God (12.32) and his seemingly shameful rejection in his execution are both identified in the phrase 'to lift up'. The lifting up of Jesus is compared to the lifting up of the serpent. The relevance of the comparison seems to lie in the assumption that everyone will have life eternal who fixes his vision on the Son of Man who is lifted up, as the Israelites who looked at the bronze image were saved from death. Several Jewish sources stressed the importance of the vision of the serpent through which God healed the people,[3]

---

[1] The opposition opinion has frequently been elaborated in recent times, e.g. by Harald Sahlin, 'Zur Typologie des Johannesevangeliums', *Uppsala Universitets Årsskrift* (1950); Jacob J. Enz, 'The Book of Exodus as a Literary Type for the Gospel of John', *JBL* 76 (1957), pp. 208–15; most recently Robert H. Smith, 'Exodus Typology in the Fourth Gospel', *JBL* 81 (1962), pp. 329–42. All authors champion a view that the Fourth Gospel is determined in its structure by a very thorough-going typology of the book of Exodus. The arguments advanced seem to me without exception very forced and many details, as well as the whole thesis, are quite unconvincing.

[2] Cf. Rudolf Bultmann, *Das Evangelium des Johannes*, 1940, p. 110.

[3] The Jewish background is, along with reference to hermetic literature, well discussed by C. H. Dodd, *The Interpretation of the Fourth Gospel*, 1954, pp. 306 f.

and for John the vision of the crucified and exalted Son of Man is the same as faith in him who gives eternal life (3.14). The little phrase 'in the wilderness' in 3.14 is, therefore, not to be stressed. The lifting up of the serpent and the saving vision are the points at issue; that this actually happened in the wilderness is more or less accidental.

In the discourse which follows John's version of the feeding of the multitude the Jews demand a miracle of Jesus which would attest to his Messianic claim. They want a miracle which would surpass the giving of the manna in the wilderness which was 'bread from heaven' (6.31). Refusing this demand, Jesus answers,

> 'Truly, truly, I say to you, it was not Moses who gave you the bread from heaven; my father gives you the true bread from heaven' (6.32).

The parallel to I Cor. 10.3 is quite apparent. But it could seem that John, wholly different from Paul, disclaims the validity of the manna tradition which gives rise to nothing but a misdirected demand and a misguided expectation on the part of the Jews.[1] However, the point of Jesus' answer is that not Moses but God was the giver of bread from heaven in the desert.[2] On the other hand, although it is acknowledged that the manna was, indeed, bread from heaven, the incident in the wilderness is clearly given a subordinate position by the clause 'My Father gives you the true bread from heaven.' The true bread is, of course, Jesus himself (6.35). In him there is more than the miraculous food of the wilderness. In him there is food which nourishes for life eternal and not only physical bread which satisfied physical hunger. The event of the wilderness is seen by John to be definitely superseded by the coming of Christ. The incident of the exodus may still have typological significance, but the type is surpassed by a new event of superior quality in the coming of the Son of God.

---

[1] This is the interpretation of R. Bultmann (*op. cit.*, p. 169), who sees in the Jews' demand the folly of measuring the revelation by human criteria and the refusal to accept God's disclosure in a form which contradicts the expectation of man.

[2] C. K. Barrett, *The Gospel according to St John*, 1955, p. 240.

V

THE PROLOGUE OF MARK

1. LITERARY AND THEMATIC UNITY OF 1.1–13

Two of the great editions of the Greek New Testament, those of Westcott and Hort and of Nestle, show the structure of the books of the New Testament not only by inserting small breaks in the text between the pericopae, but also by occasionally using larger breaks indicating the end and the beginning of coherent sections. Both editions insert a large break after Mark 1.8, thus separating the introduction to the Gospel given in the appearance of John the Baptist from the beginning of the stories about Jesus. The majority of more recent commentators, however, do not conform with this separation. On a whole, the vv. 1–13 of the first chapter are understood to be a unity.[1] The reason why this opening section is here regarded as the prologue to the Gospel cannot become clear until the end of this chapter.

Mark 1.1–13 is, first of all, marked out as a unit by the locality which is the scene for everything contained in these verses, the locality being the wilderness. In v. 3, the one crying in the wilderness introduces the theme which is picked up by the account of John the Baptist's activity 'in the wilderness' (vv. 4–8). Then Jesus is reported to make his way from Galilee to John in order to be baptized by him (vv. 9–11), and although here only the Jordan is mentioned (v. 4) to record the place at which the baptism occurred, it is clear from vv. 4 and 5 that Mark wants us to regard the Jordan baptisms as incidents in the wilderness.

K. L. Schmidt[2] has made the suggestion that the words 'in the

---

[1] The unity of 1.1–13 is upheld, e.g., by V. Taylor (*The Gospel according to St Mark*, 1957), who calls this section Mark's 'prelude to his account of the Galilean mission' (*ibid.*, p. 151). Both R. H. Lightfoot and E. Lohmeyer apply the word prologue to these verses (R. H. Lightfoot, *The Gospel Message of St Mark*, 1950, p. 17; E. Lohmeyer, *Das Evangelium des Markus*, 1937, p. 9). The subdivision of the New English Bible clearly expresses the unity of 1.1–13.

[2] K. L. Schmidt, *Der Rahmen der Geschichte Jesu*, 1919, pp. 21 f.

wilderness' (v. 4) and the whole of v. 6 are a secondary expansion of the text. He thinks two traditions about the Baptist were merged; one told of John as the preacher in the wilderness, the other knew him as the Jordan Baptist. By this hypothesis, Schmidt wants to account for the slight discrepancy in the statements concerning the locality. He remarks that vv. 4 and 5 read together certainly imply that the place where John preached and where he performed his baptisms are, to the mind of the Evangelist, identical. That is, the river is part of the wilderness scene. Schmidt thinks this reveals not only a lack of geographical knowledge on the part of Mark, but also two different sources of tradition about the Baptist which are now combined in the Evangelist's account.[1] W. Marxsen[2] has suggested v. 6 may be regarded as incorporated in the source which was used by Mark, but 'in the wilderness' (v. 4) may be a redactionary remark of the Evangelist, who wished to bind his account of John's ministry more closely to the prophetic announcement in vv. 2 and 3. In view of the fact that later on in the second Gospel the wilderness theme is repeatedly used by the Evangelist in editorial remarks (see pp. 104 f.), Marxsen's suggestion has its merits. Nevertheless, in view of the discoveries at Qumran it seems very likely that Schmidt's sensitivity regarding discrepancies in the locality is too punctilious to be true. It can now be regarded as established that the regions around the Dead Sea and the Jordan River valley were traditionally described as 'the wilderness'.[3] There is, therefore, no valid reason for regarding the phrase 'in the wilderness' in v. 4 as a redactionary addition by the Evangelist, especially since this phrase does not exhibit the characteristics of Mark's style.[4] It is certain, however, that Mark relates the baptisms in the Jordan to the wilderness.[5]

[1] K. L. Schmidt, *ibid.*, p. 21.
[2] W. Marxsen, *Der Evangelist Markus*, 2nd ed., 1959, pp. 20 f.
[3] Robert W. Funk, 'The Wilderness', *JBL* 78 (1959), pp. 209 f.
[4] Ἔρημος as a noun does not occur in the second Gospel outside the prologue. In all other places Mark uses ἔρημος τόπος and once ἐρημία (8.4).
[5] This statement is not affected by the rather confused textual evidence of 1.4. In some manuscripts βαπτίζων is linked to ἐν τῇ ἐρήμῳ by giving καί before κηρύσσων, while the text preferred by Nestle suggests taking ὁ βαπτίζων as apposition to Ἰωάννης and combining ἐν τῇ ἐρήμῳ with κηρύσσων. The reading is adopted in RSV, but, even so, there can be no doubt regarding the identification of the River Jordan with the wilderness setting.

The Prologue of Mark

After Jesus' baptism, the wilderness remains the scene for the temptation story. Thus 1.1-13 is unified by a location common to all events related in this section. In 1.14 the locality changes: Jesus leaves the desert and goes back to Galilee to begin his ministry there.

The geographical bond is not the only link which marks out 1.1-13 as a unit. Literary reasons, also, can be advanced for that view. It has been observed that Mark applies a method of stringing together traditions by the use of key-words.[1] Often larger sections in Mark can be identified by the recurrence of basic words or phrases. In 1.1-13, not only is 'wilderness' a recurring word, but also the word 'spirit'. It is used three times in this section (vv. 8, 10, 12), once each in the account of John's ministry, of Jesus' baptism, and of his temptation. The spirit theme, also, helps to knit the thirteen opening verses of the second Gospel into one whole, an observation which is made even more convincing by the fact that 'spirit of God' is a phrase otherwise only rarely used by Mark.[2]

The statement that literary links make 1.1-13 a unit does not mean that it was originally one piece of Christian tradition which was composed as a unity and so used by the Evangelist. Lohmeyer has advanced convincing reasons that at least vv. 12 f. have been an isolated tradition. He notes that in 12 f. the grammatical structure of the sentence is different from vv. 2-8 and 9-11; the subject stands at the beginning of the sentences followed by the verb and, for the first time, the historic present appears.[3] Also, the underlying conception of the spirit in vv. 10 and 12 reveals differences. In v. 10, the spirit is like an hypostasis of God, while in v. 12 it is a divine force driving Jesus into the wilderness similar to the lifting up of Old Testament prophets by the spirit (e.g. Ezek. 3.14). While Lohmeyer's observations seem to be correct, it is certain that Mark has inseparably linked together the accounts of Jesus' baptism and temptation, so that V. Taylor is

---

[1] Chiefly J. Sundwall, 'Die Zusammensetzung des Markusevangeliums', *Acta Academiae Aboensis*, Humaniora, IX (1934).

[2] Πνεῦμα ἅγιον is mentioned only three times in the whole Gospel apart from the prologue: 3.29; 12.36; 13.11. S. E. Johnson (*The Gospel according to St Mark*, 1960, p. 35) mentions the theme of the Holy Spirit as the only one binding together the three sections vv. 4-8, 9-11, and 12-13.

[3] Lohmeyer, p. 26.

justified in regarding vv. 9–13 as a single narrative so far as the intention of the Evangelist is concerned.[1]

2. THE PROPHECY

After the opening verse, the second Gospel solemnly starts with a quotation from the Old Testament. Whatever follows in the prologue is to be regarded as the fulfilment of a prophecy. The prophecy introduces two persons—the messenger who prepares the way, the one whose voice is crying in the wilderness, and the Lord who will follow, whose way is being prepared. The latter is announced in the wilderness and he will come through the desert, for in the desert only is it necessary to prepare ways and paths. In the cultivated country, roads already exist.

Lohmeyer has taken vv. 4–8 as a line by line commentary on the prophetic sayings. He has restricted this interpretation to Mark's account of John's activity, however, ending with v. 8.[2] Although in the LXX the 'Lord' in v. 3 means God, there can be no doubt that in Mark's context it signifies Christ. Otherwise Mark's slight alteration of the text of the LXX in v. 3 would make no sense. In the LXX Isa. 40.3 gives exactly the same rendering as we have in the Marcan text except that at the end it reads 'the paths of God', which is altered in Mark to 'his paths'. Mark, or more likely the source which the Evangelist followed, altered the text to make it applicable to the one who was known to the congregations as the *kyrios Christos*. The same Lord is meant in the personal pronouns twice appearing in v. 2 in the phrases 'before thy face' and 'thy way'. Therefore, it is not only the messenger and forerunner who is prophesied in vv. 2 f. and commented upon in vv. 4–8; both messenger and Lord are introduced in the prophecy whose fulfilment is unfolded in 1.1–13.

The quotation is a collection of three sayings from the Old Testament, two of which are from the prophets and one from Exodus. Verse 2 combines Ex. 23.20 with Mal. 3.1 in that the main clause 'Behold, I send my messenger before thy face' is taken verbatim from Exodus in the LXX rendering, whereas the

[1] Taylor, p. 158.
[2] Lohmeyer, p. 10.

The Prologue of Mark

second part of the verse originates in the Hebrew version of Mal. 3.1.[1]

Considering that rabbinical exegesis had already combined both verses and welded them into one, identifying the angel of the covenant referred to in Ex. 23.20 with the Elijah *redivivus* who is addressed in Mal. 3.1,[2] the first two combined sayings really melt into one in which Ex. 23.20 is the predominant part. We have, then, two quotations, one from the law and one from the prophets, the former being already interpreted and enriched according to rabbinical usage by another prophetic utterance. Ex. 23.20 and Isa. 40.3 are embedded in the wilderness tradition of the Old Testament. In Ex. 23.20 God promises to send his angel before the people on their way through the desert to the land of Canaan and in Isa. 40.3, which is quoted verbatim in Mark 1.3 with the slight modification just mentioned, the messenger announces the second exodus through the wilderness to the final delivery of God's people. In both instances the theme of the exodus is the dominant motif, and both vv. 2 and 3 in the first chapter of Mark refer to the wilderness theme, although the word ἔρημος only appears in v. 3. Thus three factors are brought to our attention at the outset of the second Gospel—the messenger, the Lord and the wilderness. It is clear, then, that the wilderness mentioned in the succeeding verses is not introduced in order to give geographical fixture to the record. Not the locality as such matters, but it is related because it is in accordance with the prophecy. This does not preclude that the Baptist actually

[1] It is controversial whether or not v. 2 should be regarded as original or as an interpolation. The surmise of an interpolation was made on the ground that Matthew and Luke in their accounts of the Baptist's activity quote only the Isaiah passage (Matt. 3.3; Luke 3.4), while both have the mixed Ex.-Mal. quotation in a different context (Matt. 11.10; Luke 7.27), and that it is hard to believe that a collection of testimonia should be introduced as a saying of the prophet Isaiah. Following the lead of Holtzmann, the interpolation theory is accepted by A. E. J. Rawlinson (p. 6), and with some hesitation by S. E. Johnson (p. 33), and V. Taylor (p. 153). Others prefer to retain the text as it stands, amongst them A. Farrer (*A Study in St Mark*, 1952, p. 55), E. Lohmeyer (p. 11), K. Stendahl (*The School of St Matthew*, 1954, p. 215). The blending of three Old Testament passages which are all related to the wilderness theme seems to me to fit so perfectly into the whole setting of the prologue that I regard v. 2 as original. If it is an interpolation, it was done most ingeniously.

[2] Lohmeyer, p. 11.

appeared in the wilderness; but the conformity to the prophecy is the point that matters to Mark. R. W. Funk[1] maintains that the two centres associated in the New Testament with John's baptisms (Bethany, John 1.28, and Aenon, John 3.23) fall within the range of the lower Jordan valley and the wilderness of Judah which are already in the Old Testament described by the word ἔρημος.[2] While the Synoptics give us no precise location, it is obvious that both Matthew and Luke are interested in a definite geographic fixture of John's activity—the former in the wilderness of Judea (3.1), the latter in all the region about the Jordan (3.3). It is all the more striking that in Mark no attempt is made to designate the precise location at all. Apparently, Matthew and Luke were not satisfied with the generality of Mark's statement. Their more precise reference to locality may or may not rest on reliable tradition. The point important to us at present is the fact that Mark is not concerned with geographical interests. The desert as such and the Jordan in general as falling within its range are the only important factors to him because they correspond to the prophecy.

The wilderness in Mark 1.3 carries with it the full weight of a great religious tradition embracing high hopes and promises as well as the deep shadows of judgment and despair, and this is imposed upon the succeeding verses, moulding them as counterparts of Israel's experience in the desert.

3. THE HERALD

Mark 1.4–8 describes the ministry of John the Baptist. The description is brief and concise. It is as though the Evangelist did not want his readers to know more about the Baptist than three things, all of which are the fulfilment of the prophecy which he put at the beginning of his Gospel: (1) John was a man in the wilderness, (2) there he performed his ministry of baptism thus preparing the way of the Lord, and (3) the announcement of the

---

[1] R. W. Funk, 'The Wilderness,' *JBL* 78 (1959).
[2] *Ibid.*, p. 210. It ought to be kept in mind, however, that the two place names in the Fourth Gospel cannot be identified with any site known to us today. See G. E. Wright and F. V. Filson, *The Westminster Atlas to the Bible*, 5th ed. (1957), p. 93.

The Prologue of Mark

one mightier than himself who was to come after him. Every detail of the five verses is related to one or more of these three points. Apart from them and the story of his death (6.14–29), John remains unknown to us in the second Gospel, in contrast to the accounts of Matthew and Luke, who have endeavoured to furnish much more information about him.

The quotation from Isa. 40.3 in v. 3 states that the messenger of the Lord will cry in the wilderness. Mark makes it clear at once that the appearance of John the Baptist is to be seen in the light of this prophecy—he did his work in the wilderness (v. 4). Whether this little phrase ἐν τῇ ἐρήμῳ was found by the Evangelist in his source, or whether he inserted it himself, makes no difference to the interpretation. In either case, 'in the wilderness' links the ministry of John with the prophetic promises—the messenger is to appear in the desert. The reference to John's clothing and food serves to underline this (v. 6). These details about the Baptist are recorded not to satisfy the curiosity of early Christians who were wondering how John might have looked and what noteworthy habits he might have had, but simply to stress the fact that he was a man of the desert. The cloak of camel hair and the use of locusts and wild honey were familiar garb and food to the wilderness nomad.[1] What is said in Mark 1.6 about John's clothing and food, therefore, 'is to be taken merely as an attempt to characterize his life in the wilderness'.[2] Only one detail in v. 6 possibly indicates more than this. John is said to have worn a leather girdle around his waist. This, according to II Kings 1.8, was also a characteristic feature of the prophet Elijah's dress, and Mark, who lays considerable stress on the interpretation of the Baptist as a second Elijah, has in all likelihood taken John's belt for an indication that John and Elijah are to be seen together.

John, the man in the wilderness, is sent to prepare the way of the Lord—so the prophecy says. The Evangelist sees the fulfilment of it in John's baptism ministry. With regard to this point, the modern reader and commentator on the Gospel alike face very considerable difficulties of understanding. In what sense can the baptism in the Jordan be the means of preparing the road for Christ? The problem is presented in Mark's description

[1] C. H. Kraeling, *John the Baptist*, 1951, pp. 10 f.
[2] *Ibid.*, p. 13.

of John's message—John preached 'a baptism of repentance for the forgiveness of sins' (1.4).

The phrase 'a baptism of repentance for the forgiveness of sins' is riddled with difficulties. It is not explained what either baptism or repentance means; apparently it is taken for granted that the reader already knows the meaning of both words. The modern interpreter, however, has to reckon with numerous possibilities. John's baptism has been explained as a symbolic sign in line with symbolic actions recorded about prophets in the Old Testament,[1] as based on the Jewish custom of proselyte baptism,[2] as a lustration rite similar to Essene practices,[3] and as manifestation of a baptism movement which adopted Iranian, mandaean or gnostic ideology.[4] The position seems to be much less complicated regarding the word repentance. It was very widely used in Judaism at the time of the New Testament. In fact, it was so much a favourite theme of rabbinical theology that G. F. Moore was able to call it 'the Jewish doctrine of salvation'.[5] Closer investigation shows, however, that the opinions concerning the nature of repentance were by no means uniform.[6] Moreover, with regard to both baptism and repentance it is not at all safe to assume that John simply perpetuated the thinking or the custom of his time. We have at least to reckon with the possibility of a great deal of originality on his part.

It will be helpful at this point to give a short résumé of two positions which are fairly representative for the main lines of approach. E. Lohmeyer, in an essay 'Zur evangelischen Überlieferung von Johannes dem Täufer'[7] and later in his commentary on Mark, has gone very far in an interpretation of baptism as an eschatological sacrament. C. H. Kraeling, on the other hand, in his book *John the Baptist*, derives the meaning of the phrase

---

[1] C. H. Kraeling, *John the Baptist*, pp. 117 f.
[2] J. Leipoldt, *Die urchristliche Taufe im Lichte der Religionsgeschichte*, 1928, p. 27; J. Jeremias, 'Der Ursprung der Johannestaufe', *ZNW* 28 (1929), pp. 312–20; H. G. Marsh, *The Origin and Significance of New Testament Baptism*, 1941, pp. 56–66.
[3] W. Brandt, *Die jüdischen Baptismen*, 1910, pp. 48–50.
[4] R. Reitzenstein, *Die Vorgeschichte der christlichen Taufe*, 1929; J. Thomas, *Le Mouvement Baptiste en Palestine et Syrie*, 1935.
[5] G. F. Moore, *Judaism* I, 1927, p. 500.
[6] Cf. J. Behm, art. μετανοέω, *TWNT* IV, pp. 987–94.
[7] In *JBL* 51 (1932), pp. 300–19.

The Prologue of Mark

entirely from contemporary Jewish thinking and gives it a predominantly ethical significance.

Lohmeyer emphasizes the fact that the phrase starts with κηρύσσων. Κηρύσσειν does not simply mean preaching, but, very specifically, the public announcement of a prophet called by God. The content of the prophet's speech, therefore, 'is not his word or wisdom but God's announcement and speech'.[1] Now, the concrete object of the divine announcement through John was baptism. Baptism, for that reason, must be understood as a work of God to which the people who were baptized subjected themselves. Baptism, then, as a work of God, cannot only be a representative action as we know it from several prophets. For then the phrase in Mark would have to read: John preached repentance in baptism and not, he preached a baptism of repentance. Further, as work of God, baptism achieves its end, which is repentance. Repentance cannot, in Mark 1.4, signify the human decision of turning one's mind to God, since a divine action cannot be determined by a human factor. Lastly, Lohmeyer argues, the words 'for the forgiveness of sins' 'can only signify the good which is grounded in baptism and not a goal which is outside baptism, for baptism is a work of God'.[2] Therefore, and this is Lohmeyer's result, baptism for the forgiveness of sins means the divine gift of turning to God which is given in the act of submersion and entailed in this is the forgiveness of sins. Baptism is 'a kind of eschatological sacrament'.[3]

It must be admitted that Lohmeyer's exegesis is based on a profound investigation into the proper meaning of each word, and especially on a serious appreciation of the word order of the phrase. C. H. Kraeling, in opposition to Lohmeyer's interpretation, arrives at his conclusion by placing the Baptist's message on the background of Jewish tradition. Kraeling says, Lohmeyer's explanation 'would actually set John's conception of

---

[1] 'Was er redet, ist nicht sein Wort und seine Weisheit, sondern Gottes Spruch und Rede'—*Das Evangelium des Markus*, p. 13.

[2] The phrase 'for the forgiveness of sins' 'kann nur ein Gut bezeichnen, das in der Taufe, nicht ein Ziel, das ausserhalb ihrer gelegen ist, ist doch Taufe ein Werk Gottes' (*ibid.*, p. 15).

[3] 'Sie is nicht ein Symbol und Gleichnis—wie könnte sie sonst Reinheit schaffen und verbürgen?—sondern eine Art eschatologischen Sakraments' (*ibid.*, p. 19).

repentance apart from anything known to contemporary Judaism'.[1] It must be noted that repentance is nowhere defined in the New Testament and the meaning could only be taken for granted, for repentance was understood in traditional terms familiar to every contemporaneous Jew. Apart from that, had baptism been a divinely inspired medium for repentance, it would be impossible to explain why Jesus did not perpetuate it after John's death. 'It seems wise, therefore, to assume that for John, repentance had the same basic meaning as for all Jews, namely, that of turning from sin in contrition and confession, and of turning to the will of God.'[2] The question remains, however, how forgiveness and baptism were associated for John. Kraeling points out that in the account of Josephus, John's baptism is described as a lustrative rite and it is denied that the rite had any connexion with the remission of sins. This apparent divergency from the statement in Mark, Kraeling suggests, is a contradiction more apparent than real. 'It can be ironed out by the assumption that Mark's words, "for the forgiveness of sins", describe not the action of the rite itself, but the action of God associated with the performance of the rite by man.'[3] Judaism produced no rite efficacious of and by itself, i.e. a sacrament, and neither was John's baptism sacramental. Repentance as an act of self-humiliation before God, however, did have divine forgiveness as its response. 'If John's baptism, then, was an act of repentance it could mediate forgiveness without conferring it.'[4]

A comparison of Lohmeyer's and Kraeling's expositions of the crucial phrase concerning the Baptist's ministry shows up the main problems of Mark 1.4. In an endeavour to come to a conclusion and, possibly, find another more satisfactory answer, the little phrase 'in the wilderness' in 1.4 can be regarded as the clue to the understanding of the whole verse. Surprisingly, interpreters have never attempted to take seriously the connexion between the baptism and the proclamation of repentance with the setting in the desert. 'In the wilderness' (1.4), of course, refers back to 1.2 f. What was announced of old has now come to pass: in the

[1] C. H. Kraeling, *op. cit.*, p. 69.
[2] *Ibid.*, p. 71.
[3] *Ibid.*, p. 121.
[4] *Ibid.*, pp. 121 f.

The Prologue of Mark

desert the decisive event in the history of God and his people has begun to unfold itself. The cross-reference between vv. 2 f. and v. 4 with regard to the wilderness has often been regarded as a purely mechanical linking together on the assumption of the fulfilment of testimonia. It may be contended, however, that this cross-reference provides the essential background for the understanding of both baptism and repentance in Mark 1.4.

It will be convenient to begin with the word repentance. We have seen, in the previous discussion, how deeply the Old Testament concept of repentance is rooted in the wilderness tradition.[1] Actually, the expectation of a renewed period in the desert was the starting-point of the prophet's message of repentance. While in orthodox Jewish circles at the time of Christ no trace of this understanding of repentance can be found,[2] the theology of the covenanters at Qumran proves that this concept was by no means extinct. There is a vigorous section of Jewish religious life at this time which understands itself as the community of the covenant of repentance, and it is at least very likely that the fact of their life in the wilderness is directly connected with their claim to be the community of penitents.[3] Stating this does not mean to aver that the Baptist was himself a member of the Qumran community. It does show, however, that an intimate correlation of the wilderness with the concept of repentance was present. The correlation was no innovation and must have been easily comprehended by the contemporaries.

This means that the Baptist's call to repentance and his call to come to him in the wilderness to be baptized are but two aspects of one and the same thing. The wilderness, according to prophetic teaching, was the place of Israel's original sonship; here God had loved his people. But, as they had fallen from their genuine filial love which they had enjoyed during their sojourn in the desert, a renewal of the exodus into the desert was necessary for the restoration

---

[1] See pp. 46 ff.

[2] Cf. art. μετανοέω by Behm in *TWNT* IV, pp. 991–4. Is it possible that all traces of a correlation between repentance and the wilderness in rabbinical theology were later on deleted when the rabbinical sayings were collected? H. J. Schoeps (*Theologie und Geschichte des Judenchristentums*) repeatedly refers to the practice of the rabbis of fighting Christian claims by deleting old rabbinical material whenever it could support Christian views.

[3] See pp. 58 ff.

of Israel's status as son of God. In this second exodus, God's revelation in power and help would be achieved again, and the prophets visualized the renewed exodus into the wilderness as the beginning of God's eschatological act. John the Baptist announces the imminence of this final act of God which will be established through the work of the one whom he prophesies. He is announced by John in the desert and he will appear in the desert to achieve his work, as it is foretold in the prophets and expected in Jewish hopes. This event is close at hand, and therefore John calls the people out to the wilderness; and the other phrase says the same thing—he calls them to repent. Going out into the wilderness and repentance are not two different ideas which could only be related to one another as form and content or as condition and result. Rather they are essentially one and the same—the march out into the wilderness *is* the repentance to which John calls.

Similarly, an immediate correlation of baptism and the wilderness theme is quite conceivable. J. Jeremias has collected rabbinical evidence[1] indicating that the reason given for proselyte baptism was found in the necessity to make the convert undergo the same experience which Israel as a people had once undergone —the passing through the Red Sea. Israel's passage through the Red Sea and under the cloud is assumed to be her baptism which is re-enacted at the baptism of the proselyte. It is established by I Cor. 10.2 that the parallel between baptism and the crossing of the Red Sea was not unknown to Christian interpretation. J. Jeremias advanced his argumentation in order to explain John's baptismal rite as having arisen from Jewish proselyte baptism. This deduction may or may not be correct. All that matters for our inquiry is the fact that the idea of baptism as a re-enactment of the event which stood at the beginning of Israel's exodus into the wilderness was possible at the time of the Baptist. It must be admitted that some other explanations of John's rite have equally much to commend them. But considering all points in the prologue of Mark, this interpretation strongly suggests itself. The appearance of the Baptist in the wilderness, his call to repentance and his baptism are thus intelligible as three aspects of the prophecy which expected the final delivery of God's people that was to take place in the desert.

[1] J. Jeremias, 'Der Ursprung der Johannestaufe'.

The Prologue of Mark

Repentance in John's kerygma is, therefore, conditioned by an action of God who is presently going to act in history in a unique and all-decisive fashion. The opportunity and the urgency of repentance are given, for the one who is to baptize with the Holy Spirit is close at hand. A final action on God's part is the basis of repentance. This understanding of שׁוּב is fully in line with Old Testament prophecy up to Jeremiah, 'return to me, for I have redeemed you' (Isa. 44.22). At the same time, of course, repentance involves action on man's part. The journey out into the wilderness, however, is farther reaching and more radical than the rabbinical understanding of repentance as contrition and confession. It must not be forgotten that to the Old Testament as a whole, and to the prophets in particular, the desert is the place of judgment. Israel has to return anew to the wilderness because she can only re-establish her position as God's beloved son by surrendering her achievements and pride. The return to the wilderness means the acknowledgment of her whole history as a history of disobedience and a willingness to begin at zero. This reduction to nothing is divine judgment acknowledged by the people of Judea and Jerusalem in the confession of their sin, but it is also the starting-point for a new history of grace. The one mightier than John will commence his work in the wilderness, and a new period of grace, the time of final revelation of the power of God, will set in. The march out to the Baptist in the wilderness is related both to the past and to the future; to the past, because it entails the acknowledgment of the futility of Israel's history and the necessity of a new beginning through judgment as it was pronounced in the Old Testament, and to the future, because it is an action performed in expectancy of an eschatological act of God through the one entitled and empowered to baptize with the Holy Spirit.

4. THE LORD

The prophetic announcements with which the Second Gospel begins not only predict the forerunner but also the Lord. Mark 1.4–8 has not introduced the Lord himself except in an anonymous way in v. 8, but as the Baptist was the visible representation of the truth and the power of the prophetic hope, so the κύριος must be made manifest to the reader of the Gospel as the fulfilment's second and greater part. The note struck in vv. 2 f. has not ceased to ring in v. 8, and v. 13 sounds the same theme.

By way of repetition: vv. 9–13 are connected to vv. 2–8 by the theme of the spirit and the wilderness as the common locality of the scenes. Mark has identified the Baptist at Jordan with the preacher in the desert, and so the mentioning of Jordan in v. 9 ensures that there is no change in scenery between vv. 8 and 12.

The quotation from the Old Testament in vv. 2 f. has left no doubt that the messenger would appear in the wilderness. As far as the way of the Lord is concerned the meaning of the words is somewhat ambiguous. It is left undecided whether he is going to use the desert as a transit only in order to further his work somewhere else, perhaps at Jerusalem, or whether he is going to be associated with the desert more permanently so that his passage through the waste land is not only a rapidly passing moment. This cannot be determined by vv. 2 f., but vv. 9–13 give an answer.

The Baptism

We have observed the close correlation of repentance and baptism with the wilderness theme. The question now arises whether this observation can be further substantiated by Mark's account of Jesus' baptism.

The Baptist had announced that the one who was stronger than he was going to baptize with the Holy Spirit (v. 8). The difference between this verse and the parallel accounts of both Matthew (3.11) and Luke (3.16) is remarkable. The other two Synoptics preserve a tradition (possibly Q) following which the Baptist expects the Messiah to baptize with Holy Spirit and fire. This is apparently in line with their tradition concerning the judging function of the Messiah (Matt. 3.12; Luke 3.17). Fire is a symbol of judgment and the Spirit can well be understood in the same way.[1] It is striking that Mark, either following a different tradition or consciously changing his source, preserves no allusion to the judging function of the Lord. J. E. Yates[2] has shown that the

---

[1] C. H. Kraeling, *op. cit.*, pp. 61 f.
[2] J. E. Yates, 'The Form of Mark 1.8b', *New Testament Studies* IV (1958), pp. 336 f. It can be argued, of course, that Mark 1.8 issues from a pre-Marcan source in which Christian interpretation contrasted the baptism of

The Prologue of Mark

Spirit in Mark is consistently understood as the agent of purification and not as an effect of baptism. Baptism with Holy Spirit is, therefore, to be regarded as the process of purification which begins with the ministry of Jesus (1.14), reveals its most obvious manifestation in the exorcisms of Jesus (3.29)[1] and comes to its head in his death.

The baptism with the Holy Spirit which the Lord is to perform stands, however, in striking contrast to the baptism which he himself undergoes (1.9). Verses 8 and 9, skilfully placed side by side, portray an enormous contrast: the giver of life here, the lowly penitent there; one active in the victorious struggle against evil on the one hand, the same man entirely passive in receiving the sign of repentance on the other. There is no passage in the Second Gospel which exposes the so-called Messianic secret in a more forceful manner than vv. 8 and 9 of the first chapter read together. Yet, the contrast is even enhanced if Mark 10.38 is also taken into consideration. The saying about the cup which Jesus is drinking and the baptism with which he is being baptized is usually interpreted as a figure of speech which signifies his death.[2] G. Delling, in a detailed analysis, has pointed out that both cup and baptism are well-established expressions in the Old Testament signifying the execution of Yahweh's wrath.[3] Βάπτισμα βαπτισθῆναι need not be understood as a technical term for baptism; it simply means to be the object of God's judgment. Mark 10.38 is accordingly not necessarily to be connected with Jesus' death alone. The

---

John with the baptism of the Church (R. Bultmann, *History of the Synoptic Tradition*, ET of 3rd ed. [1957] and Ergänzungsh. [1958], 1963, p. 246, see, however, the critique of Kraeling, *op. cit.*, p. 60). Yet this would only be applicable to the pre-Marcan state of the tradition. The assumption that the fulfilment of the prophecy 1.8 was recorded in the lost ending of Mark has the value of every theory which rests on no evidence (E. Schweizer, art. πνεῦμα, *TWNT* VI, p. 396: *Spirit of God* [BKW], p. 27).

[1] J. M. Robinson, *The Problem of History in Mark* (SBT, 21), 1957, pp. 29 f.
[2] So E. Klostermann, *Das Markusevangelium*, 2nd ed., 1926, p. 121; Lohmeyer, pp. 222 f.
[3] G. Delling, 'Βάπτισμα βαπτισθῆναι', *Novum Testamentum* II, 2 (1957), pp. 92–115. Delling's analysis shows further that Mark 10.38 consequently does not have to be interpreted as a reference to the martyrdom of the sons of Zebedee. The argument that the verse is a *vaticinium ex eventu* is in that case as invalid as the assumption that v. 38 is a secondary element (Bultmann, *History*, p. 24).

saying explains his mission as a mission to endure God's judgment which, of course, culminates in the crucifixion. Important to us is the conclusion that Jesus' mission of bearing the judgment of God can be called a baptism. We shall see later that Mark did not regard Jesus' act of repentance as terminated once and for all in the event of his baptism. This suggests that we have to look upon the saying 10.38 as the authentic interpretation of the relation of Jesus' baptism in the Jordan to his whole ministry. What was begun in the baptism of John was continued in the course of Jesus' mission, and the understanding of the mission as endurance of God's judgment in turn explains the essence of John's baptism. This baptism is the sign of the acknowledgment of God's judgment.

We have thus reached the point where the connexion of Jesus' baptism by John and the wilderness theme becomes perspicuous. John's appearance in the wilderness, his call to repentance and his baptism imply the conviction that the time has come when God will execute this last and all-decisive judgment in which a new Israel will emerge. Jesus fully acknowledges this conviction (Mark 11.30). He is himself willing to shoulder the burden of this judgment and bear it in his whole mission.

This is further strengthened by another observation. In 1.5 Mark states that *all* the country of Judea and *all* the people of Jerusalem went out to John to be baptized. Of course, seen in historical perspective, this is an exaggeration. But it is a purposeful, theologically caused exaggeration and not just a remark with 'a touch of oriental extravagance'.[1] Both Lightfoot and Lohmeyer have suggested that there is a reason for this exaggeration. Lightfoot thinks Mark wants to 'emphasize what was only to be expected at the appearance of the herald of the Messiah',[2] and Lohmeyer, arguing along the same lines, points out that according to Deutero-Isaiah's prophecy the exodus to the wilderness was a necessity to which all members of the people of God were obliged to conform.[3] This argument can further be strengthened by a reference to the speech attributed to Paul in Antioch. Paul, speaking of John, says that the Baptist proclaimed a baptism of

---

[1] Rawlinson, p. 8. Taylor (p. 155) calls the phrase 'a touch of hyperbole'.
[2] Lightfoot, p. 19.
[3] Lohmeyer, p. 15.

repentance to all the people of Israel (Acts 13.24). Early Christian theology apparently understood the Baptist's work as a divine offer which put an obligation on Israel as a whole, and this could well be reflected in Mark 1.4. However, in Acts 13, the divine offer is obviously not utilized, whereas Mark tells us that all of Judea and Jerusalem actually went out to be baptized. Something more than the necessity for all to obey God's command which is taking form in John's ministry must be presented in Mark.

Now, it can be argued that Mark 1.5 and 1.9 stand in relation to each other. Lohmeyer observes that both sentences are built in exactly the same way;[1] apparently they are meant to be corresponding verses. A deep contrast separates them, on the other hand, in two respects. In v. 5 Judea and Jerusalem are in the picture, the holy province and the sacred capital; in v. 9 Galilee, the suspect region of half-heathendom,[2] is on the scene. Also in v. 5 *all* people come forth; v. 9 introduces *one* single representative from Galilee, the only Galilean mentioned in the Second Gospel who followed the Baptist's call. So a double contrast pervades the two verses—the holy land over against the unholy province and the many over against the one. Concerning the first of these

---

[1] Lohmeyer, p. 20. 1.5: ἐξεπορεύετο —
πᾶσα ἡ Ἰουδαία χώρα καὶ οἱ Ἱεροσολυμῖται πάντες
καὶ ἐβαπτίζοντο ὑπ' αὐτοῦ ἐν τῷ Ἰορδάνῃ ποταμῷ.
1.9: ἦλθεν —
Ἰησοῦς ἀπὸ Ναζαρὲτ τῆς Γαλιλαίας —
καὶ ἐβαπτίσθη εἰς τὸν Ἰορδάνην.

[2] E. Lohmeyer (*Galiläa und Jerusalem*, 1936) undertook to show that from the beginning Palestinian Christianity comprised a group in Jerusalem and one in Galilee. Mark's Gospel is based on the traditions of the Galilean group which expected the parousia of the Lord in Galilee (Lohmeyer on Mark 16.7). Hence, in Mark, Galilee is the Christian country *par excellence*. Lohmeyer's position is further elaborated by W. Marxsen (*Der Evangelist Markus*, 2nd ed., 1959) who champions the view that the Gospel was written in Galilee (*ibid.*, p. 41). The view of these scholars is diametrically opposite to the estimate of Galilee in the eyes of contemporary Jews as a land of semi-pagans (L. E. Elliott-Binns, *Galilean Christianity* [SBT, 16], 1956, p. 13). The Galilean was a despised fool (Elliott-Binns, *ibid.*, p. 25), and Galilee was the centre of the lawless '*am ha 'aretz* (R. Meyer, art. ὄχλος, *TWNT* V, p. 590). Of course, this does not preclude a reversal of the traditional attitude in Christian circles. But the tension between Galilee and Jerusalem in the Second Gospel cannot exclusively be attributed to the existence of two Christian groups in the very early history of the Church. The antagonism of orthodox Pharisaism against Galilee is reflected in it.

contrasts, in all remaining parts of Mark's Gospel the characterization of Judea and Galilee is reversed. Jerusalem especially, as the centre of Judea, is the place which is in rebellion against the Son of Man, who was sent from God. Christ's enemies come from Jerusalem (3.22; 7.1), and Jesus' way to Jerusalem is depicted by Mark solely as his way to the Cross (10.32 f.). The lament over Jerusalem recorded in Matt. 23.37-39, although it is not found in Mark, could well have been included in the Second Gospel also. On the other hand, Galilee in Mark's Gospel is the territory where Jesus almost exclusively performs his mighty acts; from its population he calls his disciples, here he is going to appear to his believers after his resurrection (14.28; 16.7). The same reversal is significant for the other contrast. In the course of the Gospel, the 'all' of Judea and Jerusalem who came out to John to be baptized reveal themselves to be the very opposite of newborn creatures. But the one from Galilee, as the story of his baptism tells, is the one and only beloved Son of God, the only one, apparently, who truly responded to John's call in unfeigned repentance.

Mark, apparently, felt no difficulty in putting these contrasts before his readers. To him, Jesus joining the crowd of penitents needed no apologetic remarks. Matthew, already, felt the necessity of explaining why the sinless one placed himself on a level with all sinners (Matt. 3.14 f.). It is usually regarded as a sign of the more primitive thinking of the second Evangelist that this difficulty did not seem to occur to him. I submit that the opposite is true. The sequence of vv. 8 and 9 is so significant and subtle that it is impossible to think it escaped the notice of the Evangelist of the Messianic secret, and is simply the result of two conjoining pieces of tradition. Mark, by the contrast of vv. 5 and 9, already revealed his conception of the one over against the many. At later points in his Gospel he explicitly hands on the kerygmatic tradition of the Church that Christ dies for many (10.45; 14.24). He does not see Jesus as an isolated individual who is only responsible for his own righteousness. Jesus, in Mark's Gospel, is from the very beginning a member of a body of people whose heritage and predicament he shares and, like Moses (Ex. 32.32), he does not divorce himself from the sins of his people, but is bound up with them. This, then, is expressed in v. 9; the giver of

The Prologue of Mark

the baptism with the spirit of life humbles himself to receive the baptism of repentance. With the others he follows John's call to the wilderness as the place where Israel's sonship to God is to be renewed.

When Jesus' baptism has taken place, a divine testimony attests that the sonship has indeed been re-established (v. 10). Lohmeyer points out how exquisitely the coming down (καταβαίνειν) of the Spirit corresponds to the coming up (ἀναβαίνειν) of Jesus out of the water[1]—the ascending and the descending motions are combined in a moment of meeting. As this one penitent from Galilee rises out of the water a corresponding move from heaven is reported. There have been many baptisms in the Jordan and many a man and many a woman has risen after the immersion out of the river, but their ἀναβαίνειν was never answered by a καταβαίνειν from above. In their baptisms a human action was left without a responsive action on the part of God, but in the baptism of Christ God does respond.

The divine response to the baptism of the one true penitent is illustrated in the descent of the Spirit in the form of a dove and in the voice from heaven (1.10 f.). Both illustrations are intimately connected with the prophetical expectation of a new exodus into the wilderness. The representation of the Spirit in the form of a dove does not cause great problems, in view of Jewish associations between dove and spirit which are part of a large tradition in the ancient Orient.[2] Further, the absolute use of πνεῦμα in v. 10 is no longer regarded as a certain pointer to Hellenistic Christian origin,[3] as it can be found in the Qumran texts.[4] Of importance here is the fact that, as shown above (p. 52), the Old Testament associates the outpouring of the Spirit with the hope of the new exodus in the last days (Isa. 32.15; 44.3; 63.10–14). The descending

---

[1] Lohmeyer, p. 22. D. Daube (*The New Testament and Rabbinic Judaism*, 1956, pp. 111 f.) made the suggestion that the phrase 'to come up' was assimilated from Jewish proselyte baptism where it plays a decisive part, possibly referring to the frequent occurrence of the phrase in Joshua in connexion with the crossing of the Jordan. Daube's suggestion, however, fails to account for the correspondence of ἀναβαίνειν and καταβαίνειν in Mark 1.10 which seems to me the decisive point.

[2] H. Greeven, art. περιστερά, *TWNT* VI, p. 68.

[3] So Bultmann, *History*, p. 251, and Taylor, p. 160.

[4] E. Schweizer, art. πνεῦμα, *TWNT* VI, p. 397, note 430 [BKW, p. 29, note 5].

of the Spirit on Jesus on the occasion of his baptism in the wilderness is, therefore, well motivated.

The other sign is the voice from heaven, declaring Jesus to be God's beloved Son. Of all titles attributed to Jesus in the Second Gospel the term Son of God is the most significant one.[1] The words of the heavenly voice are based on Old Testament words. Ps. 2.7 and Isa. 42.1 are used, but Taylor remarks rightly that it is not a quotation and echoes other Old Testament passages.[2] At any rate, the great theme of sonship is introduced, whose vital connexion with the wilderness theology in the Old Testament has already been pointed out. In the wilderness, Israel is first designated to be the son of Yahweh (Ex. 4.22 f.; Hosea 11.1; Jer. 2.2), and in the event of Israel's return to the desert her sonship will be renewed. In Jesus the old prophecy is fulfilled. Israel is, so to speak, concentrated in the person of Jesus. What the baptism of the many did not bring about is achieved in the true penitence of the man from Galilee. Thus, his exodus into the wilderness to John is shown to be the only valid exodus. All others have only physically gone out to Jordan—they returned to their Judean homes basically unrepentant. Only Jesus fully realized what it meant to go out into the wilderness: it meant the determination to live under the judgment of God.[3]

Expulsion into the Wilderness

The story about Jesus' baptism is followed by the account of his ejection by the Spirit into the wilderness. In fact, the baptism

---

[1] Taylor, p. 120; also, Lohmeyer, p. 4.
[2] Taylor, p. 162.
[3] Essentially the same view is expressed by commentators who see in Mark 1.11 a reference to Isa. 42.1 and explain the verse as Jesus' initiation to the office of the servant of Yahweh (O. Cullmann, *Baptism in the New Testament* [SBT, 1], 1950, p. 16, and *Christology of the New Testament*, 1959, p. 66; Taylor, p. 162). Bultmann (*History*, Supplement to p. 251) regards this opinion as fantastic. The interpretation of Mark 1.11 as an adoption formula (M. Dibelius, *From Tradition to Gospel*, p. 271; R. Baultmann, p. 248; Maurice Goguel, *Jean Baptiste*, 1928, pp. 142 ff.) is impossible in view of the intention of the Evangelist. It is questionable whether this interpretation rightly characterizes the pre-Marcan tradition (see M. Barth, *Die Taufe—ein Sakrament?* 1951, p. 76; Lohmeyer, p. 23). The parallel 9.7 proves that to the Evangelist the voice from heaven did not convey the notion of adoption into a new status but of declaration and revelation.

The Prologue of Mark

story has no proper end at all and its connexion with the following vv. 12 f. is thus very close.[1]

Mark's account of Jesus' sojourn in the desert is extremely brief. The brevity of the account, and the fact that neither the content of the temptation nor the other traits of the episode are explained, has led several scholars to assume that Mark 1.12 f. is the rudiment of a richer story.[2] The basis of this argument is a comparison between the pericope in Mark and the parallels in Matthew (4.1-11) and Luke (4.1-13). In contrast to Mark, the other two Synoptics furnish us with details about the end of the temptation period. Taking Matthew and Luke as points of reference, Mark's account looks indeed like a fragment. But the question is whether Mark's brief episode is meant to be primarily a temptation story at all. M. Dibelius[3] has suggested that the real theme of these short verses is a description of Jesus' sojourn in the wilderness and all details mentioned apart from this are secondary to the main theme. Matthew and Luke singled out the temptation motif, combined it with a record about a dialogue between Jesus and Satan, found in Q, and thus created a proper temptation story. On the basis of Dibelius's argument, Mark 1.12 f. does not need to be regarded as a mutilated rudiment and the brevities of the text cease to be obscure. Moreover, if the forty days' sojourn in the wilderness is to be regarded as the primary scope of the narrative, the thematic continuity of the prologue becomes conspicuous: the Lord, announced and baptized in the wilderness, continues to be there for forty days.[4]

After the baptism, the Spirit is said to have driven Jesus out

---

[1] Taylor, p. 158; cf. Lohmeyer, p. 20.

[2] So Bultmann (p. 253), Schniewind (p. 48), J. Dupont ('L'arrière-fond biblique du récit des tentations de Jésus', *New Testament Studies* III [1956–7], pp. 294 f.).

[3] *Die Formgeschichte des Evangeliums*, 3rd ed., 1959, p. 129, in footnote. This footnote is omitted in the English translation.

[4] Perhaps the phrase τὸ πνεῦμα αὐτὸν ἐκβάλλει εἰς τὴν ἔρημον is another indication that in the pre-Marcan tradition the episode vv. 12 f. was not connected with the baptism story. Since Mark regards John's baptisms as events occurring in the wilderness, the statement of an expulsion of Jesus into the wilderness is somewhat inconsistent. How can Jesus be driven from the wilderness into the wilderness? Apparently Mark has not attempted to iron out the unevenness of his sources. This shows again that he is not interested in geographical precision. To him the wilderness is a theme full of theological implications, not primarily a locality.

into the wilderness. The driving out 'appears to indicate strong, if not violent, propulsion'.[1] The close connexion between the baptism and the wilderness story indicates that we are to regard Jesus' expulsion into the desert as the necessary outcome of his baptism: the same Spirit which descends upon him at his baptism, accompanied by the voice declaring him to be God's son, now forces him to penetrate into the wilderness even more deeply. This is of great significance. If the interpretation of John's call to repentance, given above, has been adequate, repentance is to be understood as return to the desert. The story of Jesus' baptism conveys the man from Galilee as the only true penitent whose return to the desert is unfeigned. As the true penitent he is proclaimed to be the Son of God who represents the new Israel in his decision. At this point, however, the question emerges: Is the penitence of the Son of God completed at his baptism? Is the humbling aspect of his mission terminated with his declaration as the Son of God and are we now to expect the renewal of the picture into the portrayal of his triumphant victory? The narrative of Jesus' expulsion into the desert gives the clear answer that this is not the case.[2] The penitent remains a penitent; after his baptism he does not abandon but abides in the wilderness. Moreover, so far, Mark has not explained what the desert represents. We have inferred that the move out into the wilderness was the act of repentance and, conversely, to repent meant to follow John's call to come out to him into the wilderness. What that entails we have, nevertheless, not yet been told. Mark 1.12 f. proceeds to tell us what it means to be in the wilderness, i.e. what it is to be truly repentant. It means to be confronted with Satan and his temptations, to be with the beasts and to be ministered to by angels. As they explain the main theme, these verses are the culmination of the prologue. Each detail is rooted in the wilderness tradition of the Old Testament and serves to clarify the significance of the desert.

(*a*) Jesus stays in the wilderness for forty days. This reminds

---

[1] Taylor, p. 163. The power of the Spirit to lift up the prophet and remove him to some distant place is known in the Old Testament. The similarity to II Kings 2.16 is remarkable. See also I Kings 18.12; Ezek. 8.3.

[2] Perhaps the account of the expulsion of Jesus into the desert was influenced by the story of the scapegoat in Lev. 16.7–10, 20–22. This would underline the representative character of Jesus' baptism. The suggestion was made to me by A. R. C. Leaney.

The Prologue of Mark

one immediately of Moses' stay on Mount Sinai and Elijah's wandering through the desert to Mount Horeb.[1] The forty days are a fixed time of symbolic meaning. Does Mark mean to say that at the end of this time Jesus left the wilderness, leaving behind him a period of his life which was never to be repeated? Although this seems the natural way to understand the phrase, it must be noted that in the case of both Moses and Elijah the time of the forty days serves a different function. Both of them are men of the wilderness.[2] Before and after this period of time they continue to be associated with this locality, the forty days simply concentrate into one focal period the essence of their ministry, the innermost quality of their mission is revealed in them in a figurative symbol. The same could be true of Jesus in Mark 1.12 f. We have to regard the forty days not as a period passed for ever once Christ starts his public ministry, but, as with Moses and Elijah, as the sounding of the keynote of his whole mission.

(b) The temptation is an inevitable and significant concomitant phenomenon of the wilderness. Of all the side themes of the wilderness tradition, both in the Old and New Testament, it is the most frequent one. The temptation is said to be caused by Satan.[3] Satan, or Beelzebub, is the prince of demons (3.22), i.e. the head of all powers hostile to God, who hates and destroys God's work amongst men (4.15). Jesus' determination to repent, his abiding in the wilderness, is thus explained as a clash with the personified evil. J. M. Robinson[4] has drawn attention to the cosmic language of Mark 1.9–12. What happens on the plane of human decision,

---

[1] Ex. 24.18 and I Kings 19.8, 15. Sinai and Horeb are used in the Old Testament synonymously. R. Kittel (art. ἔρημος, *TWNT* II, p. 655) has denied any relation of the forty days in Mark 1.13 to the Old Testament tradition. Against him rightly W. Schmauch, *Orte der Offenbarung und der Offenbarungsort im Neuen Testament*, p. 38.

[2] Concerning Elijah, see below, pp. 114 ff.

[3] In the wilderness tradition of the Old Testament, Satan rarely figures as tempter, it is usually God who tests his people. While the change is in part probably due to the influence of Jewish tendencies to preserve the transcendence and greatness of God, it also effects a difference in the meaning of temptation. God's tests as reported in the Old Testament are never understood to have any other but purifying and strengthening aims. In Mark 1.13 the meaning of temptation is the attempt on the part of Satan to undo God's work. Thus the influence of late Jewish thinking has considerably radicalized the issue.

[4] *The Problem of History in Mark*, pp. 26–28.

Christ in the Wilderness

namely in the Baptist's call and in Jesus' response, is at the same time revealed as a struggle between God and his counterpart. It is mostly overlooked that Mark, in contrast to Matthew (4.11) and Luke (4.13), reports neither Jesus' victory over Satan nor the end of the temptation.[1] He does not do so because, to him, Jesus did not win the victory in the forty days nor did he cease to be tempted. This does not mean, of course, that Mark wants to portray a Jesus who was overcome by Satan and fell to temptation. It strongly underlines, however, the intention of our episode: Jesus in the wilderness is confronted with Satan and temptation. It is this clash itself which is important; it is going on in Jesus' whole ministry. That explains also why Mark does not have to say anything about the content of the temptation. The whole Gospel is an explanation of how Jesus was tempted. What is paramount at this stage of the drama is simply the statement that in Jesus' response to the Baptist's call and consequently in his decision to return to the wilderness, the confrontation of the Son of God with the power of Satan takes place.

(c) The animals mentioned in Mark 1.13 have caused endless embarrassment to expositors. Since Mark 1.12 f. is usually understood as an account of Jesus' temptation, and since his victory over Satan is always assumed, the reference to the wild beasts is often interpreted as signifying the victory of the new Adam against Satan, the restoration of a paradisaical state of the world and consequently man's peace with the animals.[2] Sometimes it is observed that in the Old Testament the wilderness is said to be the place inhabited by animals hostile and frightening to man.[3] Whenever it is realized that the wilderness theme is the dominant line in the prologue of Mark, the reference to the animals ceases to be fortuitous. In the desert tradition of the Old Testament the motif of animals adverse to man is frequent.[4] They represent the

---

[1] S. E. Johnson, p. 40, speaks of the overthrow of Satan. Also Lohmeyer, p. 28, who remarks that the victory is a matter of course and could for that reason be left out, and Schniewind, p. 49.

[2] J. Jeremias, art. Ἀδάμ, *TWNT* I, p. 141; L. Goppelt, *Typos*, p. 118; Bultmann, p. 254 (as a possibility); Schniewind, p. 48.

[3] So Schniewind, p. 48.

[4] See the collection of material on p. 37. In Ps. 91.11–13 angels protect against danger from animals. The psalm was certainly in the mind of Matthew (4.6) and Luke (4.10 f.), but I doubt if this is true of Mark, cf. J. Dupont, *op. cit.*, p. 294.

The Prologue of Mark

horror and the danger which faces man in the desert. Possibly in New Testament times the animals were associated with demons.[1] They have affinity with the realm of Satan and when Jesus meets them in the wilderness he faces the horror, loneliness and danger connected with them.

(d) The angel is a familiar figure of the Old Testament wilderness stories.[2] Nearest to Mark's account is, again, 1 Kings 19.5, 7. As in this story the angels have the function of providing Jesus with nourishment in the barren waste, the only difference between the two stories being that I Kings 19 speaks of one angel and Mark gives a plurality of angels. The tendency to multiply the numbers and importance of the supernatural powers in comparison to the Old Testament is a common feature of Jewish theology. It fully accounts for this detail in Mark's presentation. But the purpose of the appearance of the angels in Mark 1.13 is the same as the guiding and helping angel during Israel's exodus. The dominant aspect of Jesus' stay in the wilderness is his temptation by the adversary of God and at the same time his sustenance by the servants of God. It must be noticed that the service of the angels, although mentioned last, is not said to terminate the temptations. Mark thinks of the temptation, the being with the animals and the service of the angels as continuous events in the course of which all the forces of God and Satan are simultaneously present.[3] This is indeed a very fitting description of the ministry of Jesus for the Evangelist, who has made the Messianic secret the guide for his presentation of the traditional material about Jesus which was in his possession.

The attempt has been made to interpret Mark 1.1–13 as a closely related unit to form the prologue of the Second Gospel. The traditional theme of the wilderness, which plays so vital a part in the Old Testament and is, as was shown, known to early

---

[1] The association of demons and wilderness animals is already observable in the Old Testament (Isa. 13.21; 34.14 LXX). Cf. Mark 5.13.

[2] Perhaps Mark wanted to refer specifically to the ἄγγελος mentioned in 1.2 taken from Ex. 23.20, who is promised by God to be Israel's guide and helper throughout the wanderings. Apart from this the angel motif is an important one in many stories of the exodus (e.g. Ex. 14.19; 23.23; 32.34; 33.2).

[3] Contrast the significant alteration in Matt. 3.11.

Christian theology, serves as the string on which the beads of tradition available to Mark for the composition of the prologue were assembled. From the opening verses restating the prophecy of the second exodus to the two parts of its fulfilment in the appearance of John the Baptist and of Jesus the Son of God, this theme is constantly preserved. As is fitting for a prologue, the hidden truth of history is once and for all revealed.

The reason for calling the section 1.1–13 the prologue of the Gospel can now be seen. It provides, as R. H. Lightfoot observed, the key to the whole Gospel by introducing the person and office of the central figure of the book before the readers.[1] Jesus' baptism and wilderness sojourn are not merely the first acts of Jesus' public appearance. They are equally the foundation of his whole ministry.[2] Through them the stage of the ensuing drama is set—the stories of Jesus' ministry can now be told. In acordance with Old Testament prophecy and determined by the call of John the Baptist, it will be a story of Jesus' temptation in his confrontation with Satan and of help from God. To live in this condition is to live in the wilderness. Now, after the presuppositions of the story are revealed, the Gospel can begin, Jesus can go into Galilee, preaching the gospel of God (1.14).

[1] R. H. Lightfoot, *The Gospel Message of St Mark*, p. 17.
[2] J. M. Robinson, *The Problem of History in Mark*, p. 31.

VI

THE WAY THROUGH THE DESERT

1. INTRODUCTORY CONSIDERATIONS

THE word wilderness (ἔρημος), or its derivations, does not occur often in the Second Gospel after the prologue. Twice in the first chapter Christ is reported to have withdrawn to a wilderness-spot (εἰς ἔρημον τόπον, 1.35; ἐπ' ἐρήμοις τόποις ἦν, 1.45). In the story of the feeding of the five thousand the same phrase occurs three times (6.31, 32, 35), and again in the parallel story of the feeding of the four thousand the ἐρημία is mentioned (8.4). The appearance of these phrases is generally in no way connected by commentators with the report about the work of John the Baptist in the wilderness. In fact, the reader of the RSV could not possibly notice any relationship between these passages. In 1.35; 6.31, 32, 35, the Marcan expression is rendered 'lonely place', in 1.45 the translation is 'he was out in the country', and only in 8.4 do we find the expression 'desert'.[1] These translations are understandable. In the phrase ἔρημος τόπος the word ἔρημος is used as an adjective, in contrast to 1.3 f. and 1.12, and so seems to carry less weight. The phrase is apparently regarded in the RSV as a reference to some solitary spot, either near Capernaum (1.35) or somewhere else in Galilee (ch. 6). Any reference to the wilderness proper in these verses must have seemed misleading to the translators, as the district around Capernaum was well cultivated at the time,[2] and the first account of the feeding of the multitude contains a reference to green grass (6.39). The underlying assumption of these translations is, of course, that the verses in question refer to certain geographical spots preserved by Christian memory as places of Christ's activity.[3] But even commentators who would be

---
[1] The New English Bible renders the phrase in question with 'lonely place' in 6.31, 32, 35, and 8.4, 'lonely spot' in 1.35, and 'open country' in 1.45, i.e. the RSV is followed at this point.
[2] Cf. E. G. Kraeling, *Bible Atlas*, p. 379.
[3] So Taylor, p. 183.

inclined to grant that the phrase ἔρημος τόπος may not furnish us with an historically reliable indication of some scene in Christ's life do not connect the wilderness passages in the main body of Mark's Gospel with the scene of the prologue.[1]

A closer analysis of the verses mentioned shows, however, that this assumption is not satisfactory. It ought to be noted, first, that the passages in Mark associated with the wilderness-place[2] belong to different strata of the tradition.

In 6.35 and 8.4 ἔρημος τόπος and ἐρημία are indispensable elements of the account of the feeding miracle and therefore must be part of the earliest tradition. Verses 1.35, 1.45 and 6.31–33, however, reveal the redactionary work of the Evangelist. Verse 1.45 is the clearest instance; more recent scholarship is agreed that at least the second half of the verse, beginning with ὥστε, gives Mark's own words.[3] Verses 1.35–39 and 6.30–33 are regarded by Bultmann as the Evangelist's work.[4] In 6.30–32 Lohmeyer and Taylor trace disconnected biographical tradition together with redactionary work.[5] Both scholars regard the unit 6.30–34 as constructed by Mark. The phrase ἔρημος τόπος is typically Marcan. Whenever Matthew follows Mark's account, he copies it (Matt. 14.13 par. Mark 6.31; Matt. 15.33 gives ἐρημία par. Mark 8.4), but in all cases when he is independent of Mark he uses the noun ἔρημος (11.7; 24.26). Luke also follows Mark's wording in 4.42 (cf. Mark 1.35). Again, whenever he is independent of the

---

[1] Taylor argues in all cases from a geographical point of view. Thus 1.35 can, to him, not mean the desert but only a lonely place, since the region of Capernaum was well cultivated (p. 183), while in reference to 6.31 he considers various topographical possibilities (p. 319). Lohmeyer sees in 1.33 and 1.45 the motif of the tension between public action and secrecy (pp. 42 and 49). Johnson (p. 50) and Rawlinson (p. 19) regard 1.35 as expressing Jesus' wish to pray in solitude. Obviously a different explanation must then be found for 1.45 and 6.31 ff. Johnson remarks in regard to 1.45 that Jesus preferred to work not openly but secretly (p. 53). Marxsen maintains that the wilderness passages in the main body of the Second Gospel are not connected with the occurrence of the theme in the prologue (p. 29).

[2] In order not to preclude the following discussion and in an attempt to render as faithfully as possible the Greek wording I shall from here on render the phrase ἔρημος τόπος in Mark usually with 'wilderness-place' or 'wilderness-spot'.

[3] Branscomb, p. 39; Bultmann, *History*, p. 212; Dibelius, *Tradition*, p. 74; Lohmeyer, p. 48; Schmidt, *Rahmen*, p. 66; Taylor, p. 190.

[4] Bultmann, *History*, pp. 155 and 244.

[5] Lohmeyer, p. 123; Taylor, p. 318.

The Way through the Desert

second Evangelist he uses ἔρημος as a noun (1.80; 8.29; 15.4). This shows that ἔρημος τόπος is typical of Mark's language. Mark 8.4, a verse from pre-Marcan tradition, has ἐρημία, and it is reasonable to suppose that in 6.35 Mark also found ἔρημος or ἐρημία in his tradition, but changed it to ἔρημος τόπος to make the account of the miracle conform with the wording of the introductory passage 6.30–34. For this reason, I assume that the phrase ἔρημος τόπος in 1.35, 1.45, and 6.31 f. originates from the Evangelist. This proves that Mark, inserting the phrase, must have a certain intention in using it.

2. FORMAL CHARACTERISTICS AND CORRELATIONS OF THE WILDERNESS PASSAGES

Mark 1.35, 1.45, and 6.31–33 have some formal characteristics in common. The verses (*a*) are always preceded by an account of preaching and the performance of a mighty deed, (*b*) represent a retreat from the crowds, and (*c*) are followed by an account of strong attraction to Jesus on the part of the people.[1]

(*a*) Verse 1.35 is preceded by an account of Jesus' activity in Capernaum. Verses 1.21–34 would seem to be intended by the Evangelist to represent the work of one day.[2] Jesus' teaching with authority (1.22, 27) and his mighty acts displayed in the healing of the man with the unclean spirit, of Peter's mother-in-law, and of the many ill persons in the evening, are the two elements which are emphasized in the report of the first day in Capernaum.

---

[1] The combination of these three elements has been especially emphasized by H. J. Ebeling (*Das Messiasgeheimnis und die Botschaft des Marcus-Evangelisten*, 1939, pp. 116 ff.).

[2] Lohmeyer's tendency to discover a threefold structure in Mark's arrangement of the tradition leads him to maintain that the passage 1.21–45 is subdivided into two main sections each consisting of three parts. 1.21–31 describes the first day in Capernaum as the day of 'the appearance of our Saviour Christ Jesus' (I Tim. 1.10; Lohmeyer, p. 34) and vv. 32–45 are marked out as a unit under the point of view of the departure from and return to Capernaum (p. 40). This analysis is forced, as vv. 32–34 have nothing to do with a thought of departure. Taylor (p. 170) and Schniewind (p. 52) regard 1.21–39 as a unit, the latter saying that it is intended to convey the impression of a day's account. But vv. 35–39 have their scope in pointing out Jesus' decision to leave Capernaum. Hence they are not a part of the description of the first day in Capernaum, but rather a relatively independent section motivating Jesus' withdrawal from the first place of his activity.

Equally, 1.45 is preceded by the report of the healing of the leper who, after the cure, goes out 'to talk freely about it, and to spread the news' (1.45).[1] The words 'to talk freely' and 'to spread the news' suggest that the healed leper does not simply tell the story of his cure. He spreads the good news and is, in a sense, the first missionary for the one who healed him.[2] Finally, 6.31–33 follows the remark concerning the return of the twelve disciples from their first missionary journey. They had been sent out by Christ to preach and to heal (6.12), and after the completion of their charge they report 'all that they had done and taught' (6.30). Thus, in all cases, an account of either Jesus' or the disciples' preaching and healing mission is found prior to the statement of the retreat into the wilderness-place.

(b) All three passages speak of a retreat. In 1.35 Jesus' move away from the people is strongly emphasized by the hendiadys 'he rose and went out'.[3] The condition of the text with regard to these two words is not quite clear, several manuscripts omitting either one or the other of them, but the omissions are easily explained as an attempt to improve the rather awkward wording of Mark as did Luke in his parallel verse 4.42. In 1.45 the retreat is even more obvious. Mark says it was the outcome of the leper's spreading the good news that Jesus 'could no longer openly enter a town', but was out in the wilderness-places (ἐπ' ἐρήμοις τόποις ἦν). We are not yet concerned with the motivation for the retreat given by Mark, but only with the fact that Jesus' return to the wilderness-spot is a withdrawal from the public. In 6.31–33 the same move is also a means of retreat, this time for the disciples. Again it is emphasized strongly in that the phrase 'into the wilderness-place' is repeated, each time accompanied by a particular stress on the solitude. The return to the waste place is a move away from the crowds so that Christ and the disciples can be 'by themselves' (κατ' ἰδίαν).

[1] J. Jeremias (*Die Gleichnisse Jesu*, 4th ed., 1956, p. 66 [ET of 3rd ed., *The Parables of Jesus*, 1954, p. 61]) regards Jesus as the subject of the sentence in 1.45. This is hardly correct.

[2] 'To proclaim' (κηρύσσειν) and to spread 'the word' (διαφημίζειν τὸν λόγον) are technical terms signifying the Christian mission (cf. Acts 8.4 f.; II Tim. 4.2).

[3] 'Ἐξῆλθεν καὶ ἀπῆλθεν has much more force than the RSV rendering. More adequate and precise is the NEB rendering 'he got up and went out. He went away to a lonely spot.'

The Way through the Desert

(*c*) The retreat to the ἔρημος τόπος is always followed by an indication that the withdrawal of Jesus and the disciples attracts the crowds to follow them out into the wild country. Verse 1.35 is different inasmuch as 'Simon and those who were with him' are the only ones who follow Jesus to his place of withdrawal (1.36). However, it is evident that the disciples, searching after their master, are only spokesmen of the population of Capernaum. They are bearers of an almost reproachful message: 'Everyone is searching for you' (1.37). It is no empty conjecture to assume that, had Jesus not gone away (1.38 f.), the crowd would have been ready to follow Peter and his companions to the wilderness-place. Verse 1.45 states the contrast concisely—Jesus is 'in the desolate places', but the 'people came to him from every quarter', and 6.33 vividly expresses the same idea—'they ran there (i.e. to the ἔρημος τόπος) on foot from all the towns, and got there ahead of them' (i.e. ahead of Jesus and the disciples).

All the passages mentioning the wilderness-place, when read in context, reveal the same structure. First, Jesus or the disciples carry out their mission of preaching and healing. Then the retreat follows, introducing an element of retardation suggestive of a deliberate withdrawal from what appears to be a successful mission. But the retreat, in turn, only causes the crowds to search out Jesus and his disciples, and thus the picture of the crowd moving out to Christ into the desolate area is effected, most clearly in the story of the feeding of the five thousand.

Thus far in this chapter no attempt has been made to define more precisely what the words ἔρημος τόπος really mean: whether they visualize simply a lonely place, whether some connotation of a wild area is included in them, or whether, indeed, the wilderness theme with its theological implications affords the real background to our understanding. A consideration of the phrase in itself can lead to no conclusion, but it is correlated with several other words and phrases, the consideration of which can help to clarify the problem. In the first place, the incident mentioned in 1.35 closely resembles two other instances in the Second Gospel, reported in 6.46 and 14.32–42. These three passages, and these alone in the Second Gospel, give an account of Jesus praying. In all cases Jesus is alone: in 1.35 in the wilderness-spot, in 6.46 on the mountains and in 14.32–42 in the garden of Gethsemane, although in the

Christ in the Wilderness

last instance he is accompanied by the three 'favourite' disciples, who are only separated from him by a little distance (14.35). In Gethsemane, Christ and the disciples are also, in fact, on a mountain, or hill, as the garden is located on the 'Mount of Olives' (14.26).[1] The three passages are, furthermore, akin as the prayer always occurs during the night. In 1.35 this is expressly stated, in 6.46 it is suggested by the following section as Jesus meets his disciples afterwards on the sea 'about the fourth watch of the night' (6.48), and in the Gethsemane story it is indicated by the fact that the preceding meal with the disciples took place 'when it was evening' (14.18). Night and solitude are the setting for Jesus' praying in Mark.[2] Twice it is located in the mountain and once it takes place in the wilderness-spot. This sugests that 'mountain' and 'wilderness-place' have some characteristics in common. Further in 6.31 f. the wild area is twice connected with the phrase 'by yourselves' or 'by themselves' (κατ' ἰδίαν), and in 9.2, at the beginning of the transfiguration story, Jesus takes the three disciples with him 'up a high mountain apart by themselves'. The interrelation of these terms may lead to a clarification of the meaning of the wilderness-place in the Second Gospel.

3. THE MOUNTAIN

The word mountain (ὄρος)[3] appears in Mark's Gospel in 11.23 in a saying of Jesus which has clearly no importance for this investigation. It is also used in 11.1, 13.3 and 14.26 to locate some incidents at a place near Jerusalem, the Mount of Olives. In these three verses a specific geographical spot is envisaged, and there-

[1] Cf. Taylor, p. 551.
[2] The remark of Euthymius concerning 6.46 χρήσιμον γὰρ ταῖς προσευχαῖς καὶ τὸ ὄρος καὶ ἡ νὺξ καὶ ἡ μόνωσις ('The mountain, night and solitude are suitable for prayer'), quoted by several exegetes (see Taylor, p. 328), is fairly typical not only for the usual interpretation of Jesus' prayer on the mountain, but also for the understanding of the meaning of ἔρημος τόπος in the view of most scholars.
[3] Cf. W. Foerster, art. ὄρος, *TWNT* V, pp. 475–86. Johannes Jeremias, *Der Gottesberg*, 1919, utilizes studies in comparative religion in the Near East undertaken by A. Jeremias. The contribution of R. Frieling, *Der Heilige Berg im Alten und Neuen Testament*, 1930, is unique. Frieling endeavours to interpret the biblical passages concerning the mountain on the basis of R. Steiner's anthroposophy. Cf. also W. Schmauch, *Orte der Offenbarung und der Offenbarungsort im Neuen Testament*, esp. pp. 69–76.

The Way through the Desert

fore it seems doubtful whether the Mount of Olives can rightly be compared to cases where a mountain in general is mentioned. However, a comparison of the places of Christ's prayer mentioned above should warn one not to judge too rashly, and it is to be noted, moreover, that in 13.3 we find again Jesus and four selected disciples together 'privately' as was reported similarly in 9.2. The Mount of Transfiguration, unidentified though it is, and the Mount of Olives may have something in common. Perhaps they are not only locations known and sacred to Christian memory, but they may share some quality which is of importance for the understanding of the Evangelist, caused by the idea of the mountain in general. Three other passages in Mark which mention the mountain shed further light on our question. In 3.13 Jesus is said to go up to the mountain to appoint twelve men to be his disciples. Here a similarity to the passages mentioning the wilderness-place can be observed. The ascent to the mountain again creates the impression of a withdrawal from the crowds. The same must be said concerning 6.46. The great feeding miracle has just been told. Then, very strangely, Jesus forces (ἠνάγκασεν) the disciples to leave the scene of the miracle (6.45) and he himself also withdraws to the mountain.[1] Unmistakably, the Evangelist wants to create the impression of a sudden, almost violent retreat, and this shows that the wilderness areas and the mountain are motifs fulfilling the same function in Mark's Gospel.[2] The last verse in question (9.2) is preceded by a section of public teaching addressed to both the multitudes and the disciples (8.34–9.1). However, the notion of a deliberate retreat from the crowd is here very vague, as 9.2 mentions six days which have elapsed after this teaching.

A survey of these passages shows that two elements are evident in Mark's usage of the word mountain. One is that the mountain serves as a place of retreat from the public, however motivated (3.13; 6.46); the other that the word is associated with moments of ultimate revelation (9.2; 13.3). The previous chapters have shown that wilderness and mountain are very often intimately correlated

---

[1] The statement of W. Schmauch (*op. cit.*, p. 73) that nowhere in Matt. and Mark is Jesus alone on the mountain is incorrect. In Mark 6.46 Jesus is definitely by himself.

[2] See also W. Schmauch, *op. cit.*, p. 62.

and the wilderness theme throughout the Bible is familiar with both elements of the mountain as they are used by Mark.[1] Mount Sinai or Horeb, the wilderness mountain of the Old Testament, is the hallowed ground for the giving of the law (Ex. 20), the establishment of the covenant (Ex. 24), and theophanies to Moses (Ex. 24.15 ff.) and Elijah (I Kings 19.9 ff.). Without being the sole place of revelation, it is the place associated with the basic revelatory event in the history of the Israelites.

Many examples show how the desolate mountain ranges of Palestine provided excellent hiding-places (Judg. 6.2; I Kings 18.4; 19.8 f.; I Macc. 2.28; 4.5; 9.38, 40; Heb. 11.38; Josephus, *De bello Judaico* I, 36). More particularly, the barren mountain regions and the wilderness can become identical. The *Martyrdom of Isaiah* mentions Isaiah's retreat 'on a mountain in a desert place' (2.8); the deserts and mountains, dens and caves of Heb. 11.38 apparently refer to one and the same characteristic locality; the Gerasene demoniac who, according to Mark 5.2, 5, 11, lives in tombs in a mountainous area, is said in Luke 8.29 to dwell in the desert; and the shepherd who leaves his sheep in the mountains in Matt. 18.12 is said to leave his flock in the wilderness in the parallel version Luke 14.4. The same identification is perhaps underlying a verse in Mark's apocalypse. In 13.14 we read, 'When you see, the desolating sacrilege set up where it ought not to be . . . then let those who are in Judea flee to the mountains.' The verse resembles the passages in Josephus (see. p. 57) where the surviving Jews after the capture of Jerusalem ask for permission to retreat to the wilderness. Mark 13.14 is probably part of a Jewish apocalypse used by Mark,[2] and the flight to the mountains in this source could suggest not only the search for a refuge, but also the withdrawal to the place where the final delivery through God was expected. If this be so, wilderness and mountain would again be identical.

The association of the mountain with the wilderness tradition is particularly evident in the story of the transfiguration, Mark

---

[1] The function of the mountain in the Bible is, to be sure, not restricted to being a place of retreat or revelation. The mountain is symbolically used to express of firmness and strength, ancient concepts of its nearness to the realm of the divine have left distinct traces particularly in the Old Testament, and in eschatological imagery it has its place. Cf. Foerster, *art. cit.*, pp. 479-86.

[2] Bultmann, *History*, pp. 122 and 129.

The Way through the Desert

9.2–8, a passage which requires more detailed consideration.[1] It has often been observed that this story recalls the account of Moses' ascent to Sinai and his vision of the glory of God (Ex. 24.12–18).[2] However, the similarities are not restricted to some isolated motifs. Every main feature of the transfiguration story finds its counterpart in the wilderness tradition of the Old Testament.[3]

(*a*) The transfiguration is introduced by the remark that it happened 'after six days' (9.2). This unusually precise temporal statement apparently refers back to the first prediction of suffering (8.31) and the ensuing teaching on the necessity of suffering (8.34–38), but more particularly to Jesus' announcement that there are some 'who will not taste death before they see the kingdom of God come with power' (9.1).[4] The vision of the three disciples corresponds to the promise that some will see (9.1), and the transfiguration is told in the terminology of a theophany which reveals the powerful coming of the kingdom of God. The phrase 'after six days' recalls Ex. 24.16 f.[5] There we read that Moses and Joshua spend six days on Mount Sinai while the cloud covers the mountain. At the end of this preparatory week, on the seventh day, the Lord calls Moses into the midst of the cloud, where he stays for forty days to receive the law. The six days in Ex. 24.16 and Mark 9.2 designate a time of preparation for the reception of revelation. Mark apparently thought that Jesus' announcement of his approaching suffering was the preparation for the disclosure of Christ's real nature.[6] Thus, the suffering and

---

[1] The transfiguration story has recently been given much consideration. A detailed account of the latest attempts to interpret this very difficult passage may be found in the introductory chapter of H. Riesenfeld's book *Jésus Transfiguré*, 1947.

[2] Cf., e.g., J. Jeremias, art. Μωυσῆς, *TWNT* IV, p. 873; Johnson, p. 155.

[3] Contrary to this view is the opinion of Bultmann, who grants the possibility that Ex. 24 may have influenced Mark 9.2–8, but denies that the story as a whole can be explained on this basis (*History*, p. 260).

[4] If the position of Mark 9.2–8, interrupting the natural continuity of 9.1 with 9.11–13 (Bultmann, *History*, p. 260), is due to redactionary arrangement, then the intention of the Evangelist is even clearer.

[5] See also Dibelius, *Formgeschichte*, p. 275, n. 5 (not translated in the English edition); J. Jeremias, *art. cit.*, p. 873; Lohmeyer, p. 173. As a possibility among others this explanation is mentioned by Johnson, p. 156, and Klostermann, p. 98.

[6] Lohmeyer, p. 174.

the glorification of Jesus are linked together at the beginning of the transfiguration story.

(*b*) Before ascending to the mountain, Jesus selects Peter, James and John as his companions and leaves the others behind. The motif of selection from a larger group is equally present in Ex. 24—Moses separates himself first from the people, taking with him only seventy elders and Aaron, Nadab and Abihu (Ex. 24.1, 9), and secondly he separates himself even from this company, Joshua only going with him further (Ex. 24.13). At the end Moses alone appears to see the glory of the Lord (Ex. 24.17 f.). It is obvious that no strict parallel can be drawn between Ex. 24 and Mark 9.2 at this point. Nevertheless, both accounts have the motif of selection in common.

(*c*) Jesus and the three ascend to a high mountain (9.2), while Moses and Joshua climb up 'into the mountain of God' (Ex. 24.1,). Since this is the point in question for our enquiry, it would yet be too early to draw any conclusions from this parallel.

(*d*) Mark 9.3 tells that Jesus was transfigured (μετεμορφώθη). Perhaps Mark's text in 9.3 is mutilated and Streeter may be right in conjecturing that the verse originally included a reference to Jesus' face gleaming with the glory of God as in Matt. 17.2 and Luke 9.29.[1] In any case, this recalls the account of Moses coming down from the mountain after the reception of the law, when he is said to have appeared with a face transformed by the vision of God's glory (Ex. 34.29). The word 'to transfigure' (μεταμορφόω) is not used in Ex. 34. On the other hand, the 'glory of God' (δόξα θεοῦ) which is a characteristic element of both Ex. 24 and 34 does not appear in Mark's terminology. II Cor. 3.12–18, a passage explicitly referring to the story of Moses' glorification on his descent from Sinai, shows, however, that both δόξα and μεταμορφόω were related words in early Christian theology which could be used interchangeably (II Cor. 3.18). Yet it must be said that while the motif of transfiguration provides a link between Moses and Christ, not every detail in Mark's narrative is accounted for by a reference to the Old Testament. Thus the description of the white clothes is manifestly dependent upon apocalyptic imagery. When the Messiah arrives he will radiate like the sun (*Test. Levi* 4.5), he will be called sun of righteousness (*Test. Judah*

[1] B. H. Streeter, *The Four Gospels*, 7th impr., 1941, pp. 315 f.

The Way through the Desert

24.1), the light of righteousness (*Test. Zeb.* 9.8) and the light of knowledge (*Test. Levi* 4.3). The 'ancient of days' in Dan. 7.9 has a raiment white as snow and, as Lohmeyer points out,[1] it must be noted that angels are often said to wear white garments in the New Testament as though this was a matter of course (e.g. Mark 16.5; John 20.12), while in the Old Testament there is no indication of this. Thus the transfiguration as such is reported about Moses and Christ, but the account in the New Testament uses a vocabulary which shows the influence of Jewish apocalyptic thought.

(*e*) On the mountain Peter suggests making three tents, an intention glossed by Mark 'for he did not know what to say' (9.6). The tent of meeting (Ex. 27.21) or tent of the testimony (Num. 9.15) is the meeting-place of Yahweh and Moses during Israel's wilderness period. In it Moses receives God's continued directions (Ex. 33.7 ff.) while the cloud, being at the same time the indication of the presence and the concealment of God's glory, assures Yahweh's continuous presence during the desert sojourn. Peter's answer to the revelation which he had just seen is intelligible on this ground and perhaps also the numinous fear of the disciples (Mark 9.6; cf. Ex. 34.30). Peter thinks it is good to be there because he knows he stands among personages of a heavenly quality who mediate the kingdom of God to earth, and he suggests erecting tents because he wishes duration for the presence of these heavenly men so that again there may be 'tents of meeting' between the realm of heaven and the sphere of earth.[2] It is this wish for duration which qualifies his answer to the vision as a

[1] Lohmeyer, p. 175.
[2] Riesenfeld (*Jésus Transfiguré*) maintains that the transfiguration story is to be understood on the background of Jewish thinking concerning the enthronement of the Messiah which was celebrated during the Feast of Tabernacles. Originally the tent was the place of divine nuptials (p. 152) and the enthronement was at the same time a wedding celebration (p. 160). During the feast Yahweh dwells in the tent (p. 176) and so the idea developed that the Messiah would also live in a booth (p. 257). The occurrence of several motifs appearing in the exodus story such as the glory of God, the cloud and the tent are thought to be projections of experiences originally located in the cult (pp. 98 f., 131, 147). But Riesenfeld's presupposition that the Feast of Tabernacles was the *Sitz im Leben* of the historical accounts of the exodus as well as of the enthronement of the Messiah cannot be proved. If this premise falls, however, his whole interpretation of the transfiguration as Jesus' enthronement as Messiah is without support.

misunderstanding. What he saw was the mystery of the resurrection (9.9), a disclosure of what was going to be the vindication of the glory of God far superseding the glory revealed at Mount Sinai.

(*f*) Mark 9.7 speaks of a cloud and a voice out of a cloud. The cloud is, again, one of the characteristics of the wilderness tradition.[1] In Ex. 24.16 it covers the mountain of God and during the whole time of the exodus it is the visible form of the governing, guiding and yet hidden form of Yahweh's presence. The voice out of the cloud is also mentioned in Ex. 24.16. The words of the voice in Mark 9.7 are for the most part identical with the voice at Jesus' baptism (1.11). Only 'thou art' is changed into 'this is' and the last part of the sentence is altered into 'listen to him'. The phrase 'listen to him' (ἀκούετε αὐτοῦ) is an allusion to Deut. 18.15 where Moses says: 'The Lord your God will raise up for you a prophet like me from among you, from your brethren—him you shall heed' (αὐτοῦ ἀκούσεσθε). Jesus is designated as the one who, according to Jewish belief, is the second Moses.[2]

(*g*) The story Mark 9.2–8 contains one more important trait—Elijah and Moses appear on the mountain and talk to Jesus (9.4). The combination of Elijah and Moses has always presented a puzzling question to commentators. Some regard Elijah and Moses as men who had not died but been lifted up to God.[3] However, while traces of a Jewish belief regarding the assumption of the living Moses to heaven can be found, they are very scanty.[4] A return of Moses and Elijah as precursors of the Messiah is not attested in old rabbinical literature. It can be said with reasonable certainty, however, that 'Moses and Elijah are the representatives of the Law and the Prophets respectively'.[5] But it would seem to be possible to go a step further. If the wilderness tradition was the element shaping the character of the transfiguration story as a

---

[1] The correlation of cloud and voice strongly recalls the wilderness tradition of the Israelites. Of course, the cloud is not only rooted in the exodus stories of the Old Testament. It has its place also in theophanies, and in the belief in Yahweh's creation (cf. Oepke, art. νεφέλη, *TWNT* IV, pp. 907 f.). The voice of God is also found in many other traditions of the Old Testament. As far as I can see, however, the correlation of cloud and voice is significant for and unique in the exodus stories of the Pentateuch.

[2] J. Jeremias, art. Μωυσῆς, *TWNT* IV, pp. 860 f.

[3] Cf. Klostermann, p. 99.

[4] J. Jeremias, *art. cit.*, p. 859.

[5] Taylor, p. 390.

The Way through the Desert

whole, there is a perfectly natural explanation possible for the combined witness of Elijah and Moses. Both of them are men of the wilderness *par excellence*. Concerning Moses, this statement is self-explanatory; regarding Elijah, it is less obvious and requires justification.

During his lifetime it seems to be taken for granted that Elijah lives in a desolate region. After his ascension to heaven, his successor Elisha is asked to send fifty men to seek Elijah in a lonely unknown spot (II Kings 2.16)—apparently this is the natural place to seek him. It is remarkable that in this context we have a phrase which closely resembles Mark's account of Jesus' expulsion into the wilderness. In II Kings 2.16 Elijah is said to be caught up by the Spirit of the Lord and cast upon some mountain or into some valley, and in Mark 1.12 Jesus is cast out by the Spirit into the wilderness. The mountain and the valley of II Kings 2.16 and the wilderness of Mark 1.12 denote the same wilderness-like area. Frequently, Elijah is forced to retreat to this area. The account in I Kings 19.4–8 shows him in flight from the wrath of Jezebel, the queen, who threatens his life. He retreats into the wilderness, despairing of his mission (v. 4), and is there miraculously sustained by God through the service of an angel (vv. 5–7). In a passage resembling the above, Elijah is reported to seek safety from the anger of King Ahab and departs to a region east of the Jordan at the brook Cherith (I Kings 17.3–6). No mention of the desert is here made, but obviously a lonely and wilderness-like area must be meant, as Elijah is, again, wonderfully nourished through the help of ravens which bring bread and meat. In yet another passage we are told how a hundred prophets escape the plots of the queen by hiding in caves and are sustained there by the help of Obadiah, a servant of the king (I Kings 18.4). The caves were probably in those mountainous, lonely wilds which could not be populated because they afforded no means of nourishment. Elijah himself is also in such a cave on Mount Horeb (I Kings 19.9). In fact, he seems to be in an almost permanent condition of retreat to some wastelands, so that nobody knows his whereabouts. Only when God calls him to deliver a message to the royal house of Samaria does he leave his hiding-place. Then he is to 'go down' to the king, meaning that he is to leave his refuge in the solitary mountains (II Kings 1.9).

As prophets in the wilderness Elijah and Moses are companions of Jesus whose work was inaugurated in the wilderness at the baptism of John and whose way, driven by the Spirit, was to be a way through the desert. The great men of the wilderness stand by his side, testifying to the character of his life and mission as the wanderer through the wilderness.

These observations indicate a striking similarity between the transfiguration story and the wilderness tradition, particularly in Ex. 24. It is also clear that, while the thematic background of Mark 9.2–8 is throughout very closely akin to the theophany on Sinai, the actual wording of our passage reveals the influence of later Jewish thought. It must also be admitted that almost every detail of this pericope can be explained with reference to traditions other than the stories of the exodus. It is, e.g., impossible to decide *a priori* that the statement about the six days in Mark 9.2 is an echo of Ex. 24.16. Taken by itself it could equally well refer to Peter's confession,[1] to the six days between the day of atonement and the Feast of Tabernacles in the Jewish calendar,[2] or to the crucifixion or resurrection.[3] The decision depends on one's opinion concerning the structure and the content of the passage as a whole. Considering the transfiguration story in its entirety, however, it must be stressed that every motif appearing in it can consistently be traced back to the reports centred round the theophany to Moses during the exodus. This is not the case with any other tradition in the Old Testament or in Jewish thinking contemporaneous with the New Testament. Riesenfeld, for example, having made an exhaustive study of the relationship of our passage to the Feast of Tabernacles, has come to the conclusion that Jesus' transfiguration must be understood as a Messianic enthronement which was celebrated at this feast. He has to concede, however, that several motifs of the New Testament account cannot find their explanation from this background.[4] An explanation which

---

[1] Taylor, p. 388.

[2] Riesenfeld, *op. cit.*, p. 276 f.

[3] M. Goguel, *Jean-Baptiste*, pp. 212–14; C. E. Carlston, 'Transfiguration and Resurrection', *JBL* 80 (Sept. 1961), p. 236. Bultmann, with some reservations, also states this possibility (*History*, p. 260).

[4] With regard to Moses and Elijah, Riesenfeld admits that he has to abandon his usual method of explaining all motifs from one common tradition (*ibid.*, p. 255). The same is true of the motif of the voice from the cloud (p. 250).

endeavours to be consistent with the characteristic combination of motifs in Mark 9.2–8 cannot but acknowledge the decisive influence of the wilderness tradition on the Gospel narrative.

If this is so, there can be no question that the high mountain (Mark 9.2) recalls the theophanies on Sinai (Ex. 24) and on Horeb (I Kings 19). In the Old Testament Sinai and Horeb are identical.[1] Sinai is several times specifically said to be located in the wilderness (e.g. Ex. 19.1 f.). and so is Horeb (Ex. 3.1). The mountain of the theophanies is a wilderness mountain. Since the high mountain of the transfiguration is the counterpart of the mountain of God in the wilderness, the correlation of mountain and desert which can be observed in other contexts in the Second Gospel is further strengthened.

If the wilderness tradition provides the background for all motifs in the transfiguration narrative, it is natural to assume that the meaning of this pericope is equally determined by this tradition. The function of Moses and Elijah in this story is neither to predict the resurrection nor to forecast the parousia of Christ.[2] Rather their role is to reveal the character of Jesus as the one in whom the prediction of the second exodus becomes a reality. The epiphany of the glory of God is an indispensable element of the desert tradition. In the case of both Moses and Elijah it serves as divine vindication of their mission during their life in the wilderness. The same is true of Jesus. His mission had started with his baptism in the desert. There the voice of God had declared him to be his beloved son (1.11). Now, at the transfiguration on the wilderness mountain, this voice is heard again and the metamorphosis is the revelation of the hidden quality of Jesus' life. The lonely Galilean understands John's call to repentance as the call to a life of persistence in the desert. The obedience to this call is now vindicated by God on the way through the wilderness. To be sure, the way through the wilderness has not yet reached its termination in the transfiguration. This precisely is the misunderstanding of Peter who, in suggesting that tents be erected, implies that he regards the time as fulfilled and the goal of the eternal

---

[1] The name Horeb is mostly used in the Deuteronomic literature, while Sinai is the traditional name in other parts of the Old Testament, particularly in the Sinai tradition in Exodus. See M. Noth, *Exodus*, p. 32.

[2] The latter is the view of G. H. Boobyer, *St Mark and the Transfiguration Story*, 1944.

sabbath as accomplished. But the position of the transfiguration between the first prediction of suffering (8.31) and the dialogue between Jesus and the disciples on the way down from the mountain (9.11–13) makes it quite clear that Peter's words in 9.5 reflect the same wrong concept as his answer in 8.32. The time in the wilderness has not yet come to an end, rather it is still to culminate in Jesus' suffering and death. The interpretation of Luke in his version of the transfiguration is therefore fully in keeping with the intention of Mark when the third Evangelist notes that Moses and Elijah spoke to Jesus 'of his departure (τὴν ἔξοδον αὐτοῦ), which he was going to accomplish in Jerusalem' (Luke 9.31).[1] For the first time, therefore, we get the impression that the wilderness theme in Mark is related to Jesus' passion. It may well be that Moses and Elijah are not only to be taken as the prophets in the wilderness, but also perhaps even more specifically as representatives of the suffering servant.[2] Moses is called the servant of the Lord forty times in the Old Testament,[3] and perhaps Elijah is also referred to in this manner in Ecclus. 48.10.[4]

This investigation into the significance of the mountain passages in the Second Gospel shows that in most cases when the mountain is mentioned the reference is not primarily topographical. Rather, an idea is expressed full of theological implications. The association with the wilderness undergirds these passages. In 3.13 and 6.46 the mountain serves the same function as the wilderness-place and in 9.2–8 it is the New Testament counterpart of the mountain of God in the desert. Taking all this

---

[1] J. Mánek ('The New Exodus in the Books of Luke', *Novum Testamentum* II, 1 [1957], pp. 8–23) interprets the ἔξοδος of Luke 9.31 as Jesus' leaving the sepulchre, the realm of death, and not, as is usually done, as his death (p. 12). He is not very consistent, however, calling Jesus' suffering, death and resurrection also the new exodus (p. 12). The possible relation of Luke 9.31 with the second exodus is also mentioned by A. R. C. Leaney, *The Gospel according to St Luke*, 1958, p. 167.

[2] J. Jeremias, art. Μωυσῆς, *TWNT* IV, pp. 825 ff., has suggested the possibility that a Jewish tradition existed at the time of the New Testament which contained the idea of the suffering, death and resurrection after three and a half days of the second Moses and Elijah (cf. *TWNT* II, pp. 941 ff.), but the existence of this tradition is a conjecture, which is, however, plausible. See also Riesenfeld, *op. cit.*, p. 262.

[3] G. von Rad, *Theologie des Alten Testaments* II, p. 273.

[4] Cf. J. Jeremias, art. παῖς θεοῦ, *TWNT* V, p. 685: trans. *The Servant of God* (SBT, 20), 1957, p. 57.

into account, it becomes possible that Mark reported the incidents on the Mount of Olives with a similar overtone. In 13.3 ff. the Mount of Olives is the scene of eschatological revelation and in 14.32 ff. the associations with the themes of the wilderness are also evident (see pp. 128 ff). The result is that the verses concerning the wilderness-place and the mountain must be seen in the same light, as they reflect a common tradition.

4. THE PHRASE κατ' ἰδίαν AND THE PARABLES

Passages mentioning the mountain are twice connected with the phrase κατ' ἰδίαν[1] in the Second Gospel (9.2, 13.3; possibly also 14.33). Whenever Mark uses the phrase the same ideas are present as in the case of the wilderness-spot or the mountain. The word 'alone' is always connected with a passage indicating either a retreat or a special revelation and in some instances the two elements are joined together. In 6.31 f., where Jesus retreats for some time to a desolate area with the disciples, the word 'alone' displays the combination of these elements. The disciples are compelled by Jesus to withdraw from the multitude after their report of their missionary journey. But the impression of a withdrawal is not the only intention of the Evangelist. The feeding of the five thousand follows, a story central to the section 6.30–8.26. Twice in this section a miracle of feeding is related (6.35–44; 8.1–10) and the word 'bread' provides a pervading theme (6.52; 7.2; 7.28; 8.14 ff.). The misunderstanding of the disciples is explained in terms of their incapacity to understand the significance of the feeding miracles (6.52; 8.17 ff.). This implies that the miracles of the loaves and fishes have revelatory significance for Mark and, therefore, the 'alone' in 6.31 f. is also meant to prepare for a passage containing important teaching. The miracle, of course, takes place in the midst of the multitude, but there is no indication in Mark that the crowds even realized what was happening. Only the disciples are reproached for their inability to apprehend the meaning of the events.

This suggests that Mark understood the stories of the miraculous nourishment in the same way as the parables. Both the

[1] For lack of a better word κατ' ἰδίαν will be rendered in the following discussion with 'alone'.

teaching in parables and the giving of bread are events in which the crowds and the disciples partake, but only the disciples are supposed to hear and see what is really taking place. So the 'alone' reappears in passages interpreting the import of Jesus' teaching in parables (4.10 with the similar expression κατὰ μόνας; 4.33 f.). In the parables Jesus unfolds 'the secret of the kingdom of God' (4.10). Every listener to his parables hears the same words, but their true meaning enshrines a mystery, the mystery of the kingdom, and when the mystery is disclosed to the disciples it happens when they are 'alone'. This esoteric note involves the aspect of withdrawal from the general public as well as the facet of special revelation. Some healing narratives display the same characteristics (with κατ' ἰδίαν, 7.33, 9.28; without κατ' ἰδίαν, 5.37, 40). The idea of a special revelation reserved even to the selected three or four among the disciples is evident in 9.2 and 13.3.

Mark's understanding of the parables presents the key to what he intends to convey in the phrase κατ' ἰδίαν. The crucial passage is 4.10–12. Probably vv. 10 and 13 were connected in Mark's source, and vv. 11–12, a saying which shows Palestinian origin and was not originally related to the parables, was inserted by the Evangelist at this point in order to introduce his concept of the parables.[1] This analysis emphasizes the importance of vv. 11 f.

In 4.11 f. two classes of people are distinguished who are confronted with one event, but the event has an entirely different meaning to each class. The one event which both classes experience is 'everything' (τὰ πάντα), but the disciples (ὑμεῖς) are enabled to see in it 'the secret of the kingdom of God', while the other group (τοῖς ἔξω) can see nothing but parables. Τὰ πάντα cannot be limited to the parables alone. It describes the event of Christ's mission as a whole,[2] but Mark applies it to the parables,

---

[1] J. Jeremias, *Die Gleichnisse Jesu*, 4th ed., 1956, pp. 7 ff. (ET, pp. 11 ff.); T. W. Manson, *The Teaching of Jesus*, 2nd ed., 1951, p. 76; Taylor, p. 255.; J. Gnilka, *Die Verstockung Israels*, 1961, p. 58. W. Marxsen, 'Redaktionsgeschichtliche Erklärung der sogenannten Parabeltheorie des Markus', *ZTK* 52 (1955), p. 262.
[2] Ch. Masson, *Les Paraboles de Marc IV*, 1945, p. 28. J. Jeremias (*op. cit.*, p. 10 [ET, p. 14]) paraphrases Mark 4.11b 'to those who are outside is everything a riddle'.

The Way through the Desert

which are thus an aspect of the whole.[1] On the other hand, then, the parables can serve as an illuminating side of the entire event of Christ's coming: everything can become a 'parable'.[2] Mark has inserted the isolated saying (vv. 11 f.) in order to show that in his view the parable is not merely a certain method of teaching—the *mashal* familiar to a Jewish audience[3]—rather, the word 'parable' is expressive of an aspect of revelation and of human understanding confronted with the revelation. The revelation of God itself has its history whenever it enters the human scene. This is the point of the explanation (4.14–20) given to the parable of the sower (4.2–9). The explanation is secondary in character and cannot be part of the original sayings of Jesus.[4] Nevertheless, Mark gives it as an example intended to show how and why the parable is to the disciples a revelation of the mysteries of the kingdom and to those outside a cause of offence. In the explanation the seed is the word (4.14). '*Logos*' is a technical term for the Christian message circumscribing in a word the entirety of God's revelation in Christ (e.g. Acts 4.4), and the whole explanation revolves around the history which the word encounters upon its impact on the world. There are those in whom Satan immediately annihilates the power of the word (4.15); those who at first accept it, but fall away in tribulations and persecutions (4.16 f.); those who also accept it, but the care of worldly concerns chokes the word (4.18 f.), and finally those who bring the word to fruition (4.20). This says that Christ's work in word and deed (τὰ πάντα) is conditioned in its effect on man by man's attitude. Verses 4.11 f.

---

[1] J. Gnilka (*op. cit.*, p. 26) recognizes that Mark 4.11 f. represents an isolated saying the scope of which cannot be restricted to the parables alone. But he goes on to say that Mark by placing the logion in its present context deprived it of its original range of meaning, restricting it to the parables (*ibid.*, p. 29). Thus, in Gnilka's view, an originally comprehensive logion became limited by its insertion into a specific context. Would the reverse process not be equally possible, that the wide meaning of the saying elevates the context to a level on which it did not stand originally? Gnilka himself comes to the conclusion (p. 83) that Mark 4.11 f. and 4.34 are, in the intention of the Evangelist, not restricted to chapter 4.

[2] J. Jeremias (*ibid.*, p. 10 [ET, pp. 13 f.]) remarks that παραβολή in Mark 4.11 f. cannot have the meaning of 'parable'. The parallelism of 11a and 11b requires one to understand παραβολή as the counterpart of μυστήριον which enforces the meaning 'riddle', 'enigma'.

[3] For a discussion of the *mashal* see Manson, *op. cit.*, pp. 59 ff.

[4] C. H. Dodd, *The Parables of the Kingdom*, rev. ed., 1950, pp. 13 f.; J. Jeremias, *op. cit.*, pp. 7 and 65 ff. (ET, pp. 11 and 61 ff.).

distinguish only two groups, vv. 15-20 distinguish four. But in comparing the two sections, the ones ἔξω are represented by the first three groups of the explanation (4.15-19), while the disciples are identical with the last group in v. 20. To all those who have no lasting adherence to the word, Christ's mission is a parable.

What, then, does parable mean in this context? In 3.23 and 12.1 Jesus addresses the scribes 'in parables'. In both instances the meaning of the words is entirely clear. While the speech 12.1-11 at least shows the formal characteristics of the *mashal*, the words in 3.24 ff. are straightforward and to the point, and if the saying about the house divided in itself could be taken as parabolic clothing of a truth, it would have to be said that the explanation of the 'parable' is given alongside it in the words referring to Satan. Consequently, in 12.12 the scribes understand the meaning of the parable very well: 'They perceived that he had told the parable against them.' Equally, in contrast to 4.11, the disciples are placed on the same level with the scribes in that they do not 'understand' the parables. In 7.17 they are said to ask Jesus about the 'parable' which refers to his teaching on ritual cleanliness. There is absolutely nothing in Jesus' words preceding the disciples' question, which is in any way difficult to understand, and consequently Christ's answer only reiterates and amplifies what he had said before (7.18-23). This infers that neither the scribes' nor the disciples' misunderstanding is due to the parabolic form of the teaching in itself. It is not due to the obscurity of the words, but to the hardness of heart of the scribes (3.5) and the disciples (6.52; 8.17), which makes them see and not perceive and hear and not understand (4.12). Therefore, a parable in Mark's understanding is not a certain form of teaching, only understandable to the initiated; the word rather describes the fate of revelation faced with the understanding of man with the hardened heart—disbelief makes everything a 'parable', a riddle, an element wholly alien to the view of man. Of course, Mark used traditions representing proper parables in the literary sense of the word, but he used the word παραβολή to express a theological idea.

Although Christ explains the parables to his disciples (4.34), it is evident that his explanations are of no avail. Continually the disciples are said to misunderstand (6.52; 7.17; 8.17 f.). The explanation of the parable of the sower (4.14-20) states the reason

The Way through the Desert

for this misunderstanding. Satan, tribulations, persecutions and care for possessions are the causes of the hardening of the heart. Especially the first two of these causes are of interest to our enquiry. Satan is the force with whom Jesus battled at the outset of his ministry (1.13), and tribulation and persecution are powers closely associated with temptation.[1] In the wilderness Jesus is confronted with the devil and temptation; conversely, whenever the power of Satan and his temptation are manifest the nature of the desert becomes operative. Those forces are overcome by Jesus, but their power is at work in the disciples (8.33). The unwillingness to endure tribulation and persecution, the care for security in the world—in one word, the unwillingness to suffer, is the real cause of the disciples' blindness. They have not grasped that to be a disciple is equivalent to losing one's life (8.35). Hence their dispute regarding who might be the greatest among them (9.34), their contempt for children (10.13), James' and John's request to sit at Christ's right and left hand in his kingdom (10.37), and finally their flight from Jesus (14.50). We have here another indication that the wilderness theme is correlated in the Second Gospel with the theme of suffering. In the desert Jesus faces Satan and the power of temptation. More will have to be said about the concept of temptation later (see pp. 128 ff), but it is already evident that temptation for Mark consists in the first place in the force which the fear of suffering exercises over man. Therefore, Jesus' determination to persist in the desert, expressed in the prologue, finds its conclusion in his decision to suffer and to die. On the other hand, the disciples are scared away from a proper understanding of their master through fear of enduring evil. They wish to evade the wilderness which is the home of temptation. Their lives are not marked by the decisive beginning which in the prologue was described as the commencement of Christ's mission. The basic cause of their disbelief is their determination to run away from the desert. This is at the same time the cause that makes everything in Jesus' work and word, his total mission, a 'parable', a riddle. The event of revelation itself is thus the cause of man's offence (4.12).

[1] Θλῖψις and διωγμός in Mark 4.17 are contracted to πειρασμός in the parallel Luke 8.13. Lohmeyer (*Das Vater-Unser*, 3rd ed., 1952, p. 138) states that temptation can become a synonym of tribulation and persecution.

In the light of this it becomes clear that the passages in Mark containing the phrase 'alone' deal either with an instruction about the necessity of suffering or about the life-giving power of Christ, for the power of life is but the secret of suffering (8.35). The transfiguration before the three disciples 'alone' (9.2) discloses the unity of both elements—the sufferer is the glorified Son of God. The pervading theme of the apocalypse, given to disciples 'alone' (13.3), is the necessity of suffering in the last times. The warning against dread of suffering in the explanation of the parable of the sower is addressed to the disciples 'alone' (4.10, cf. 4.34). On the other hand, the vivifying force of the one who 'must suffer many things' (8.31) is revealed 'alone' to the selected few in the raising of Jairus's daughter (5.37, 40) and in the healing of the deaf mute (7.33).

5. THE SEA

There is another word in the Second Gospel indicating a locality which serves as a place of withdrawal, namely the sea (θάλασσα). In 2.13 the word appears in an editorial sentence[1] connecting the story of the man sick of the palsy with the following section beginning with the call of Levi. The verse indicates a striking change of locality. In 2.1–12 Jesus is in Capernaum, and in 2.14 he must again be in a town or village, for the office of the tax-gatherer does not, of course, stand isolated at the sea. But 2.13 creates the impression that Jesus is away from inhabited places— the people come to him (cf. 1.45). In 2.1–12 Jesus is pictured in public, in 2.13 he is away from human habitation, and in 2.14 ff. he is back in a populated region. His going out 'beside the sea' thus indicates a withdrawal from the public to a lonely region and this suggests that the 'sea' has a function similar to the wilderness-place and the mountain. Moreover, the report of the healing of the sick man ends with the people's praising God. The retreat, then, again follows an account of a victory in Christ's ministry.

Mark 3.7 points in the same direction. After the healing of the man with the withered hand and the dispute with the Pharisees, Jesus is said to withdraw with his disciples to the sea. As 3.6 announces the intention of Jesus' enemies to destroy him, the

[1] See Taylor, p. 201.

The Way through the Desert

withdrawal can be taken as a flight from danger. However, it is hard to understand how the seashore would provide a safe hiding-place, and it is, therefore, more likely that Mark wants to state a withdrawal from the public throng to the solitary scene of the lakeside.[1] Verses 2.13 and 3.7 have in common that they follow the account of a twofold victory of Jesus. In both the preceding narratives a sick man is healed and the objecting enemies are silenced. In the first story (2.1–12) this is only implied, but in the case of 3.1–5 it is expressly stated 'they were silent' (3.4). Since the command 'be silent' is also found in a narrative closely resembling exorcisms (4.39),[2] the silencing of the enemies suggests that Jesus won the battle against the powers of evil which are at work in his adversaries.[3]

Another observation may further clarify the point. In 1.16–20 and 3.13–19, the calling of disciples is related; in 1.16–20 the calling of the first four followers, and in 3.13–19 the selection of the twelve. Both passages are preceded by a summary statement about Jesus' ministry (1.14 f.; 3.7–12). The summary statement in each case stands at the beginning of a larger division of the Gospel and each time the calling of the disciples is the first incident reported.[4] This reveals a conscious plan on the part of the Evangelist and makes it possible to compare his statements concerning the locality of the incidents. In 1.16–20 it is the sea, in 3.13–19 it is the mountain which is stated as the place of the calling. This further strengthens the affinity of the 'sea' with the similar motifs of the wilderness and the mountain.

Taken by themselves, the sea passages mentioned so far are not too conclusive. The correlation between the themes could be merely coincidental. Yet there is still another element in Mark's narratives about the sea which lifts the significance of the verses hitherto mentioned to a much higher plane and definitely suggests

---

[1] Taylor, p. 226. A. Farrer (*A Study in St Mark*, 1952, pp. 77 ff.) suggested that Jesus' withdrawal from the Pharisees to the lake recalls Moses' flight from Pharaoh to the sea. He also accounts for the position of the calling of the twelve in Mark 3.13 ff. by saying that 'after the Red Sea Moses came to Mt Sinai. The next scene of the Gospel must be a Sinai covenant' (p. 81). A typology to that extent seems to me unwarranted by the text.

[2] The word used in both 3.4 and 4.39 is σιωπάω. It is rendered in 4.39 in the RSV with the command 'Peace!'

[3] Cf. J. M. Robinson, *The Problem of History in Mark*, p. 45.

[4] Taylor, p. 107.

Christ in the Wilderness

a firm connexion with the wilderness theme. In two pericopes the sea displays the characteristics of a demoniac element—4.35–41 and 6.45–50. At the beginning of both stories a withdrawal from the people is indicated which is achieved by a crossing of the lake (4.36; 6.45). In both narratives a storm threatens both ship and crew. The first of the two stories shows definite characteristics familiar from the accounts of Jesus' encounter with demons.[1] Jesus rebukes the wind (ἐπετίμησεν 4.39); ἐπιτιμάω is used to express Jesus' superior command to demons in 1.25, 3.12 and 9.25. The sea is enjoined to obey in the words 'silent! be still!' (σιώπα, πεφίμωσο), again reminiscent of the terms in a demon story (φιμώθητι 1.25). The sea obeys as the demons obey and the result is a great stillness (4.39). It is certainly no coincidence that in the Marcan order the narrative of the tempest is followed by the story of the healing of the Gerasene demoniac.[2] Some parallels in these stories are both too obvious and too subtle to be the result of chance. The howling sea corresponds to the raging fury of the demoniac who cannot be tamed even by the strongest fetters, and the great stillness of wind and water after Jesus' words is like the peace of the healed man sitting clothed and sane.[3] It is strange also that the sea, which in 4.35–41 threatens to become the grave of Jesus and his followers, actually does become the burial-place of the demons who, driven into the swine, plunge into the water with their hosts (5.13). It is as though, under Jesus' command, the forces of death devour each other while they are powerless facing the Son of God.

The second sea miracle does not so clearly reveal similarities with the demon stories, the storm in this case apparently not being so severe as in 4.35. However, the association can still be observed. The disciples see in Jesus a ghost (φάντασμα, 6.49), walking towards them on the sea. It is noteworthy that Syriac Sinaiticus

---

[1] This is observed by most commentators—cf. Johnson, p. 98; Lohmeyer, pp. 91 f.; Schniewind, p. 85; Taylor, p. 275.

[2] Lohmeyer (p. 89) observes that the three (or four) miracles in the section 4.35–5.43 reveal Jesus' lordship over sea and wind, the demons and death. The arrangement of the stories is undoubtedly the result of conscious deliberation, whether it was done by Mark himself or whether the Evangelist took it over from a source. This suggests strongly that the sea, demons and death are regarded as powers hostile to God. The similarity of this thinking with that of the Old Testament lies close to the surface.

[3] So Johnson, p. 97, and Robinson, *ibid.*, pp. 39 ff.

The Way through the Desert

reads δαιμόνιον in 6.49 instead of φάντασμα, and there are stories about the appearance of ghosts on the sea in Jewish literature.[1] Apparently the sea, like the desert, was regarded as a dwelling-place for demons.

Thus in the two miracle stories 4.35–41 and 6.45–50 the sea is regarded as a demon. The cosmic struggle in which Jesus is engaged[2] brings him into conflict with the life-threatening power of nature. It is evident that in these stories the sea is understood as in the Old Testament; it is the manifestation of the realm of death. Consequently, most commentators refer to passages in the psalms where this concept is most vividly expressed.[3] We have seen in Chapter II that in the Old Testament the wilderness is closely akin to this notion of the sea (see p. 42). Only the motif of the demons is not found there. The tendency of Jewish thinking in the centuries preceding Christ to enhance the transcendence of God and to deepen the dualism between heaven and earth has resulted in the belief in mediating creatures. The concept of angels is greatly enlarged, Satan plays a far more important role, and the demons, relatively unimportant in the Old Testament, assume a strong position in Jewish thought.[4] Hence, the manifestations of chaos and death become in New Testament times dwelling-places for the demons. This is true both of the wilderness (see pp. 100 f.) and of the sea. This suggests that Jesus' retreats to the sea are related in Mark's view to his withdrawals to the desolate areas. It must be said, of course, that Jesus' appearance at the sea will in some cases have been rooted in the pre-Marcan tradition.[5] But in 2.13 and 3.7 he uses the motif in redactionary verses, each time clearly indicating a retreat. The remark in 2.13 is so abrupt and unnatural, disjoining rather than uniting the two traditions preserved in 2.1–12 and 2.14, that it must be motivated by a certain intention on the part of the Evangelist. If an intention must be assumed, however, it is bound to be the same as the one

[1] Lohmeyer, p. 134.
[2] Cf. J. M. Robinson, *ibid.*, pp. 35 ff.
[3] Johnson, p. 97; Schniewind, p. 85. Taylor (p. 272) regards the reference to psalms as unconvincing.
[4] R. Kittel, art. ἄγγελος, *TWNT* I, pp. 79–81. W. Foerster, art. διάβολος, *TWNT* II, pp. 74–78; art. σατανᾶς, *TWNT* VII, pp. 152–6; and art. δαίμων, *TWNT* II, pp. 12–16.
[5] The references to the crossing of the sea merely indicate a change of scene and belong to a different category (5.21; 6.32, 53; 8.10, 13).

which is at work in the wilderness passages, for the formal characteristics of these passages are the same. This leads to the conclusion that the retreats to the sea, at least in 2.13 and 3.7, have nothing to do with idyllic, peaceful scenery. Rather they are approaches to the realm which discloses its real nature in the sea miracles. The withdrawals to the wilderness area and to the sea are deliberate moves into the sphere of forces which manifest hostility toward God and are, therefore, the battleground for the Son of God who has come to destroy them.

6. TEMPTATION

The passages associating Jesus with the wilderness-place, the mountain, and the sea occur almost exclusively before the turning-point of the Second Gospel in 8.27. There is, nevertheless, a section in the account of Jesus' suffering in Jerusalem which displays definite affinities to the wilderness theme. The section in question is the story of Jesus in Gethsemane, Mark 14.32–42. One point of contact between the Gethsemane story and Jesus' association with the wilderness has already been referred to—only in 1.35, 6.46 and 14.32 ff. is Jesus' prayer mentioned in circumstances bearing very close resemblance (see pp. 107 f.). The similarity of the setting and the order which the Evangelist attributed to the three passages at the beginning, at a decisive point in the middle, and at the end of the Gospel—all this implies that Mark saw in these incidents fundamental events for the understanding of Jesus' life.

The Gethsemane narrative contains words which are so closely related that they may be regarded as synonyms in the context. Jesus prays that the cup (ποτήριον) may be removed from him (14.36), or in indirect speech, that 'the hour (ὥρα) might pass from him' (14.35). The 'cup' and the 'hour' are apparently expressions denoting the same idea. In 14.38 a very similar phrase is introduced; the disciples are to watch and to pray that they may not enter (ἔλθητε) into 'temptation' (πειρασμός). As Jesus asks that the hour may pass (παρέλθῃ) and that the cup may be removed (παρένεγκε), so the disciples ought to pray that they may not enter temptation. The verbs 'to pass' and 'to be removed' are evidently correlated with the 'entering' into temptation. From this it may be inferred that 'temptation' is here meant to denote the same event as 'cup' or 'hour'.[1]

Jesus and his disciples together are involved in the threat of a disaster of which Jesus alone seems to be conscious. The impending catastrophe can be called the 'hour,' the 'cup' or 'temptation'. 'Hour' is the only word which is explained more fully in the context—it is the hour when the Son of man is handed over into the hands of sinners (14.41). This is the portent and the horror of the hour, that the Son of man, who so far has always been victorious over sin and all its representatives, is going to be defeated by the sinners. The word 'cup' reveals the same connotations. It is used often in the Old Testament as a symbol of God's judgment (e.g. Jer. 25.15; Isa. 51.17; Ezek. 23.33). Jesus sees that he is to drink the cup of God's wrath, and this explains why his soul is 'very sorrowful, even to death' (14.34). The moment is approaching when the power of sin breaks loose on him and destroys him. This is the moment of temptation. Temptation is here, as in the fifth petition of the Lord's prayer, not the time of testing for the pious, but the sphere of Satanic power and the time of his dominion against which there is no protection. This leads to the question how the temptation of 1.13 is related to the temptation in 14.38. Usually, 1.12 f. is interpreted in the light of the parallel accounts in Matthew and Luke, and the little section in Mark is similarly called the temptation story. If this was the case, it would have to be said that the ideas of temptation in 1.13 and in 14.38 are very different. Mark 1.13 would be one of many examples describing how the righteous is tested, while 14.38 displays an understanding of temptation as the time and the realm in which Satan reigns. It was suggested, however, that the main theme of 1.12 f. is not the temptation but Jesus' sojourn in the wilderness (see pp. 97 ff.). The temptation is only a subsidiary element belonging to the wilderness theme. Moreover, a temptation in the sense of a test is not reported by Mark. All he does say

---

[1] Bultmann (*History*, p. 268) and Dibelius '(Gethsemane', *Botschaft und Geschichte*, 1953, p. 263) regard Mark 14.38 as a saying originally independent of the context. This is probably correct, but it needs to be explained why Mark introduced the saying at this point. He did it because he wanted to characterize the Gethsemane incident as temptation, and the saying referring to prayer and vigilance fitted well at this point. Thus the idea of πειρασμός is approximated to the one expressed in ποτήριον and ὥρα.

is that Jesus was in and through the wilderness confronted with the power of Satan. Of course, this involves the possibility of failure, and thus the association with temptation in the normal sense of the word is quickly established. But it is not the power of Jesus to overcome evil which is stressed by Mark in 1.13, otherwise a victory over Satan would certainly have been told. In the prologue, the Evangelist simply sets the stage—Jesus and Satan are going to be the main actors in the commencing drama and their encounter alone is the fact emphasized in 1.13. Now, at the end of the drama, the main characters are still engaged in battle, and temptation is still the name of their clash. But the word has now assumed a decidedly sinister tone; it is clear that in this last encounter the devil's power is going to carry the day—the hour when the Son of man is delivered into the hands of sinners is Satan's hour, because the sinners are his instruments. So far in the Gospel Jesus has been continuously confronted by the representatives of Satan, but he has always been victorious over them.[1] This means that he has continously lived in temptation, but now the situation changes radically inasmuch as the representatives of Satan achieve the upper hand. This moment is the situation of temptation beyond comparison.

The statement that in Mark Jesus' whole ministry is an incessant temptation requires further clarification. This character of Jesus' work is particularly evident in the exorcism narratives which form so basic an element of the Second Gospel. Jesus' first act of healing is the cure of a man possessed by an unclean spirit (1.23–26); the exorcisms are given an outstanding place in Mark's summaries (1.39; 3.11 f.), and the disciples are also charged to drive out the unclean spirits (3.15; 6.7).[2] The power (ἐξουσία) of Jesus is in the first place a power over demons. The discourse with the scribes in 3.22–30 makes it clear that in driving out demons Jesus is engaged in battle with the 'prince of demons' (3.22),

[1] J. M. Robinson (*The Problem of History in Mark*) has convincingly pointed out that Mark understands Jesus' whole mission as an encounter with Satanic forces. In the Marcan introduction (1.1–13) this is expressed in cosmic terms which could seem 'introductory to "war in heaven"' (p. 33), and the struggle which is here expressed 'continues in the exorcisms of the Marcan narrative' (p. 30). The struggle is also continued in the debates both with the enemies of Jesus and with the disciples (pp. 43 ff.).

[2] The words 'demon' and 'unclean spirit' are evidently interchangeable; cf. 3.22 with 3.30.

whom he has bound and whose house he now plunders (3.27). That is to say, the encounter with Satan, reported in 1.13 in terms of temptation, is being carried out in the struggle with demons. However, Jesus' dealings with men are also an encounter with the same force. It is deeply significant that whenever Mark speaks of man in general he attributes to the word a negative tone denoting the creature in disobedience to God.[1] Both Jesus' enemies and his disciples are representatives of mankind as the creature in rebellion against God. Living with them, Jesus lives virtually in confrontation with Satan and therefore in temptation. The discourses of Jesus and his enemies resemble in some of their characteristics the exorcism narratives[2] and it is to be understood in the light of this that several times the discourses are introduced by the remark that Jesus was tempted by the scribes and the Pharisees (8.11; 10.2; 12.15). The disciples are also throughout the Gospel depicted as a group of men who, in spite of their selection by their Lord and in spite of the authority given to them, misunderstand their master. They have no faith (4.40), they do not perceive the signs (6.52; 7.18; 8.17, 21), they belong to the 'faithless generation' (9.18). Peter, who is often portrayed as the leader and spokesman of the group (3.16; 10.28), is also the representative of misconceptions (1.36; 9.5 f.), and on his reply to Jesus' first prediction of suffering he is called Satan (8.33). The subsequent behaviour of the disciples shows that Peter was not alone in this attitude (9.34; 10.37), they are all 'not on the side of God, but of men' (8.33). The forthright appellation of Peter as Satan is not a

[1] Of all the verses containing the word ἄνθρωπος in the Second Gospel, the phrase υἱὸς τοῦ ἀνθρώπου must, of course, be ruled out. In the remaining instances the singular either means an unnamed individual (1.23; 3.1, 3, 5; 4.26; 5.2, 8; 12.1; 13.34; 14.13, 71), or it is used as a term describing man in general as a creature of God (2.27; 7.11, 15. 18, 20; 10.7, 9). In nearly all cases when the plural ἄνθρωποι is used, the word assumes a critical meaning: in 1.17 the disciples are ἁλεεῖς ἀνθρώπων i.e. they are to call some to be members of God's people out of the mass which is alien to God; 3.28 refers to the sins of men; 7.7 f. mentions the precepts and traditions of men in a clearly derogatory way; 8.27 speaks of the opinions of men about Jesus which all fall short of the truth; 8.33 τὰ τῶν ἀνθρώπων is an antithetic phrase to τὰ τοῦ θεοῦ; in 9.31 the υἱὸς τοῦ ἀνθρώπου is contrasted with his evil counterpart, the ἄνθρωποι (cf. 14.41); in 10.27 the possibilities παρὰ ἀνθρώποις are set against the possibility παρὰ θεῷ; in 11.30, 32 the alternative is ἐξ οὐρανοῦ ἢ ἐξ ἀνθρώπων. Only in 11.2 and 12.14 is no negative element discernible in the use of the plural ἄνθρωποι.

[2] J. M. Robinson, op. cit., pp. 43 ff.

hyperbolic figure of speech. Through the lack of faith on the part of the disciples, Jesus meets the insinuation of evil even in the very midst of his followers.

Thus Jesus' way from the beginning of his ministry to Gethsemane is depicted in the Second Gospel as an uninterrupted confrontation with the devil's might. His way is, indeed, a way of temptation and the statement of the prologue is verified—he is driven by the spirit into the wilderness, tempted by Satan. This whole way is characterized by Christ's victory over evil, but at the end the confrontation assumes a deadly aspect. The hour has come when the Son of man falls into the hands of the sinners and is thus handed over to the power of evil, which in his crucifixion seems to be triumphant over him. The way through the desert seems to come to an end in a grave, as did the march of the rebellious Israel in the wilderness.

7. THE FOLLOWERS

In the preceding pages the attempt has been made to understand some of Mark's topographical remarks as vitally influenced by the wilderness tradition of Israel. The waste places, the mountains and the sea are all tied together by the underlying concept of Jesus fulfilling his ministry in the wilderness in confrontation with the powers of Satan.

We have observed that the passages mentioning the wilderness area reveal without exception the element of the crowds pressing forward to Jesus in his place of withdrawal (see p. 107). The same movement on the part of the multitudes is evident in passages concerning the sea (2.13 f.; 3.7 f.; 4.11; 5.21). This causes the impression that the crowd follows Jesus out into the wilderness-spots or to the lake shore. This movement recalls the account of the ministry of John the Baptist. The Evangelist reports how 'all the country of Judea and all the people of Jerusalem' went out to John into the wilderness (1.5). Mark's summary statement on the effect of Jesus' ministry (3.7 ff.) tells of a similar movement out to Jesus, but clearly the response to his ministry is pictured as far exceeding that to the one of the Baptist. Hence, Jesus, who fulfils his minstry in the wilderness, is joined by his followers; the outlines of a picture emerge in which the followers are seen to be the people in whom the exodus into the wilderness takes place.

There is one section in the Second Gospel which would seem to verify this impression. It is the account of the sending out of the twelve (6.7–13) and of the feeding of the five thousand (6.30–44).[1] In 6.30 the Evangelist has firmly connected the two units of the tradition which are interrupted by the narrative about the death of the Baptist (6.14–29). The instruction given to the twelve at the beginning of their journey consists of two parts (6.8–9 and 10–11). Whether or not commentators regard these verses as derived by Mark from Q,[2] the opinion is almost universal that Matthew and Luke represent the prohibitions of vv. 8 f. in a more rigid and therefore more original form.[3] However, this is not certain at all. Mark differs from Matthew mainly in that he allows staff and sandals to be used by the disciples on their journey and the difference seems to be conveniently explained by Mark's intention to adapt more primitive Palestinian rules to the necessities of missionary work in the Greco-Roman world.[4] Judgments like this overlook the striking similarity of Mark 6.8 f. to Ex. 12.11 where the Israelites on the eve of the exodus from Egypt are commanded to eat the Passover in haste, 'your loins girded, your sandals on your feet, and your staff in your hand'. Mark 6.8 f. appears to recall this command and thus may well represent a tradition independent of the other Synoptics. If this assumption is correct, the missionary instruction to the disciples is given in accordance with the instruction given to Israel at the outset of her wanderings through the desert. The injunction to the disciples to carry neither bread nor bag, which is simply the bread container,[5] can consequently be understood in analogy to the wilderness situation of Israel. As Israel was fed in the desert with manna which she could not herself provide, so

---

[1] The feeding miracle in 8.1–10 must be regarded as a parallel to 6.30–44. The question whether the first is meant to be a feeding of Jews and the second one of the Gentiles (e.g. Taylor, p. 357) or whether both narratives are intended to represent Gentiles (e.g. G. H. Boobyer, 'The Miracles of the Loaves and Gentiles in St Mark's Gospel', *SJT* 6 [1953], pp. 77–87) is of no consequence for our discussion.

[2] Bultmann, *History*, p. 145, and Schniewind, p. 92, regard Mark 6.8 ff. as dependent on Q. Contrary, Streeter, *The Four Gospels*, p. 190.

[3] Johnson, p. 166; Lohmeyer, p. 114; Taylor, p. 304.

[4] So Bultmann, *History*, p. 145, and Johnson, p. 155.

[5] Cf. W. Michaelis, art. πήρα, *TWNT* VI, p. 121.

the disciples are to be kept alive with nourishment for which they do not have to take thought themselves.

Mark has unmistakably established a connexion between the disciples' journey and the feeding of the five thousand by his transitional remarks in 6.30–34. Here the wilderness theme is obvious; twice the retreat 'into the wilderness-place' is emphasized (6.31 f.). It is necessary to look more closely at this introduction to the feeding narrative. Mark has prefaced the feeding miracle by two small sections, one describing the return of the disciples and their rest in a solitary place (vv. 30–32), the other telling of the gathering of the multitudes and Jesus' compassion on them (vv. 33–34).[1] An attempt will now be made to show that both introductory passages are thematically united.

In the first passage, the significant point is Jesus' admonition 'rest a while' (ἀναπαύσασθε ὀλίγον, 6.31). The reference to a well-deserved rest after the strain of the journey seems to be perfectly natural. However, the word ἀναπαύεσθαι occurs once more in the Second Gospel (14.41), and this verse shows that the allusion to physical exhaustion, while not to be excluded in either passage, is at the same time expressive of a spiritual condition. In the context of the Gethsemane story to 'rest' (ἀναπαύεσθαι) corresponds to 'sleep' (καθεύδειν)—14.37, 40, 41—which is, in turn, the contrast to 'watch' and 'pray' (γρηγορεῖν, προσεύχεσθαι 14.34, 37, 38). To 'watch' is used to describe the wakefulness of Christians expecting the eschatological hour (13.35, 37), and so the physical wakefulness demanded of the disciples is only an outward expression of a vigilance which is to express itself in prayer. Likewise, the sleep overcoming the three in Gethsemane is a figure of their spiritual slothfulness and failure. The 'rest' in 14.41 is, therefore, not simply a reference to natural rest of sleep. It bears out a condition which, at the time when the 'hour' has come, reveals sinful indolence. In 6.31, in pointed contrast to 14.41, Jesus allows the disciples to rest. In correlation to 14.41 this verse assumes much greater significance than a mere reference to physical recovery. The great sign of the feeding of the multitude is about to happen and Mark leaves us in no doubt that he regards Jesus as knowing beforehand what is to come (6.37). The hour of the feeding in the wilderness is in every respect opposite to the hour of Gethsemane.

[1] Lohmeyer, pp. 122 f.

The Way through the Desert

While in Gethsemane Satan has command over the moment, the evening of the feeding miracle is a time when the glory of the Son of God appears. This difference explains the contrast of 6.31 and 14.41; when the devil works there is no time to rest, but the epiphany of the Son of God gives to the time the character of rest. This rest is found in the wilderness. We have seen that the promise of rest is a recurring theme in the wilderness tradition, both in the Old and the New Testaments (see pp. 33, 41 and 73 f.). Originally pertaining to the promise of inheriting land in Canaan, the idea was spiritualized and connected with the second exodus in which Israel is going to find her final rest (Isa. 63.14; Jer. 31.2). This promise of old is now fulfilled; the time of rest in the wilderness has come when the Son of God establishes the communion of a meal with his people.

The second introductory passage, describing the thronging of the people to Jesus and his compassion on them (vv. 33 f.), contains allusions to Num. 27.17 and Ezek. 34.5 saying that the people were 'like sheep without a shepherd'. While the shepherd motif occurs in various different meanings in the Old Testament,[1] it must be noticed that in the context of both passages mentioned it belongs to the wilderness theme. In Num. 27.17 Moses, having been told that he is to die outside the promised land (27.12–14), asks Yahweh to appoint a leader in his stead so that the congregation 'may not be as sheep which have no shepherd'. The man appointed in his place is Joshua. It will be his task to lead Israel out of the wilderness into Canaan, the land of the 'rest'. In Ezek. 34 the shepherd motif is equally tied to the wilderness theme (see p. 50 n.). It is significant that in this chapter not only the lack of a shepherd of the sheep is decried, but also the coming of a faithful shepherd, 'my servant David', is announced (34.23), who will establish a covenant of peace so that Israel 'may dwell securely in the wilderness' (34.25). Jesus is seen in Mark 6.34 on the background of these passages. He is the divinely appointed leader in the wilderness (is the identity of his name with Joshua's only coincidence?), and the issue of the house of David who gives the people security in the desert.

The introductory passage Mark 6.30–34 may contain scattered bits of tradition available to Mark, but as a whole it is certainly

[1] Cf. J. Jeremias, art. ποιμήν, *TWNT* VI, pp. 486 f.

redactionary.[1] This shows again that the wilderness theme is consciously used by the Evangelist and, more important, it gives a clue to the way in which Mark himself understood the feeding of the five thousand. The introduction indicates that in the feeding the event takes place in which the eschatological 'rest' of Israel in the wilderness is established by the Messiah.[2] The association with the wilderness idea is strongly emphasized by Mark by his twice mentioning the location 'in the wilderness-place' (vv. 31 f.). The clumsy repetition seems at first sight due to a lack of literary refinement on the part of the Evangelist. In reality it is caused by his wish to underline an element which constitutes the proper understanding of the following narrative. However, the association of our theme with the narrative did not originate in Mark's interpretation; rather it is a part of the story itself. Two details in the narrative seem to indicate this.

First of all there is the remark that the multitude was made to sit down 'upon the green grass' (6.39). The reference to the fresh pasture in the spring season is not in itself a contradiction to the Evangelist's insistence that the event took place in the wilderness. The concept of the wilderness area is so broad that it can include pastures sufficient for the grazing of flocks (see p. 18). And yet the vivid description is so striking that a reason for it must be extant. Mark's introduction (vv. 30–34) may furnish the solution. Both parts of the introduction take up a certain aspect of the wilderness tradition which is especially powerful in the prophets —the metamorphosis of the desert under God's power into a place of refreshment, life, and joy. Usually in the tradition the desert is the opposite of what it is described in Mark 6.30–34. It is the place where man is restless and haunted (Job 30.1–8); Canaan, the land of rest, begins beyond its boundaries. Equally the wilderness is the area where the sheep are scattered (Ezek. 34.6). But in the last days the land of curse will be turned into a land of blessing; paradoxically there will be rest in it and there the sheep will be collected and abundantly fed (Ezek. 34.26 f., 29) by their true shepherd. Thus the wilderness will be turned into fat pasture and

[1] Dibelius, *Tradition*, p. 75; Bultmann, *History*, p. 244; Lohmeyer, p. 123; Taylor, p. 318.
[2] The interpretation of the feeding miracle as an anticipation of the eschatological banquet was proposed chiefly by A. Schweitzer, *The Quest of the Historical Jesus*, 2nd ed., 1911, pp. 374 f.

it is probably the shepherd motif which prompted the allusion to Ps. 23.1 in Mark 6.39. Thus, the green grass, far from being an indication of the season or a novelistic detail, is an indication of the eschatological change of the wilderness into the land of fertility and rest.

Secondly, there is the strange precision in the account of the peoples' grouping on the grass. 'He commanded them all to sit down by companies upon the green grass. So they sat down in groups, by hundreds and by fifties' (6.39 f.). This arrangement reminds us of the order of the Mosaic camp in the wilderness (e.g. Ex. 18.21), although in the references in the Pentateuch the subdivision is more elaborate. The Qumran manuscripts show that this division of the camp can assume the meaning of the order of the people assembled in the desert in expectation of the eschatological event (see pp. 60 f.). If this concept underlies Mark 6.39 f., the multitude is characterized as the recipient of the Messianic grace which comes to pass in the desert consummating the second exodus.

It has often been said that the feeding narrative recalls the manna miracle.[1] In view of the Johannine tradition (John 6.31–33) and the rabbinical theory that the manna miracle was to be repeated by the Messiah, this explanation has much to recommend it. However, it would seem that the narrative handed on by Mark as well as his introductory remarks point to a broader usage of the wilderness theme. There is nothing which directly suggests a reference to the giving of the manna apart from the obvious point of the miraculous feeding and the wilderness location. If the observations advanced above are correct, the narrative is meant to be more than a mechanical repetition of the manna story. The idea of rest in the desert, the shepherd motif, and the giving of food are united elements of the wilderness tradition, all pointing toward the eschatological fulfilment of the second exodus which became reality in the epiphany of the Son of God.

The story of the feeding in the wilderness does not stand isolated in the gospel; it is connected on the one hand with the prologue and on the other with the last supper.[2] The one who was declared the Son of God in the wilderness baptism reveals his

[1] Following D. F. Strauss, e.g. Lohmeyer, p. 128, and Johnson, p. 122.
[2] Johnson, pp. 121 f.

glory in the desert. But at the beginning of his way he is alone. Of course, many more are baptized with him by John. Yet *his* course alone is confirmed as a way through the desert by his expulsion through the spirit into the wilderness. Now, carrying out his ministry, he has his followers around him. They follow him out into the waste areas and become the recipients of his might. The allusions to the last supper are apparent in the narrative itself.[1] What happened in the both feedings of the multitudes is an anticipation of the last meal in which Jesus establishes his lasting communion with his disciples and which, in turn, is an anticipation of the final consummation of the communion in the kingdom of God (14.25). Perhaps the form of Jesus' words at the last supper in the Second Gospel is another indication of the strength of the wilderness tradition in the circles from which Mark's Gospel issued. While the version preserved by Paul clearly refers to Jeremiah's prophecy of the new covenant in the words 'this cup is the new covenant in my blood' (I Cor. 11.25), the Marcan version instead speaks of 'the blood of the covenant, which is poured out for many' (14.24)—an equally clear reference to the establishment of the Mosaic covenant in the wilderness (Ex. 24.8). This is in keeping with the opinion of Mark that the last supper was a Passover meal (14.12). To him the institution of the last supper is to be understood in analogy to the establishment of the covenant of Moses.

8. CONCLUSIONS

The previous discussions have shown that the wilderness passages in the Second Gospel are structurally and thematically related to two other locations—the mountain and the sea. Moreover, the characteristic phrase κατ' ἰδίαν is connected with both the wilderness and the mountain and plays a similar role in the Gospel. A summary of the observations advanced in this chapter can now be made and an interpretation of the result can be attempted.

All passages referring to the wilderness in Mark display a threefold function. They follow a statement of the teaching and

---

[1] The praying gesture of Jesus and the breaking of the bread (6.41) is reminiscent of the last supper (14.22). Cf. Dibelius, *Tradition*, pp. 77 and 95; Johnson, p. 124; Lohmeyer, p. 127; Rawlinson, p. 85; Taylor, p. 324.

The Way through the Desert

healing ministry of Jesus or his disciples in which a victorious battle against Satanic forces takes place; they imply always a withdrawal from the scene of activity; and they are followed by an indication of the overpowering attraction of the multitudes to Jesus. These three points can be traced equally in the sections dealing with the mountain and the sea, and this similarity not only establishes a general connexion of motifs, but gives the clue to a more precise explanation of the wilderness theme.

(*a*) Concerning the first point—the preceding statement of success—both mountain and sea reveal the same function. In 3.13 and 6.46 mountain passages are clearly preceded by accounts of Christ's successful ministry, and in 2.13 and 3.7 this is evidently also the case in verses mentioning the sea. The problem arises, however, whether the other sections of the Gospel referring to either mountain or sea fall in line with this characteristic. In 9.2, 13.3 and 14.32 a mountain is said to be the location of events or of discourses which seemingly do not follow a report of Jesus' success. On the contrary, the mountain is here following in the wake of the announcement of suffering and destruction—the transfiguration story follows the first passion prediction and the sayings on the necessity of sacrifice; the apocalyptic discourse comes after the prophecy of the destruction of the temple; and the Gethsemane story is preceded by the announcement of the slaying of the shepherd of Israel and the dissipation of the flock (14.27). But both the transfiguration and the Gethsemane stories are ingrained with vital elements of the wilderness theme. In the former the Son of Man is vindicated as the victor in the desert and in the latter the concept of temptation receives its final depth. The work of Jesus which in one aspect consists in his triumphant fight against the forces of evil through his ministry of healing and teaching contains also the other aspect of his vicarious suffering. These aspects can neither be separated nor opposed to each other. Jesus' ministry unites them in indissoluble unity. Both are equally the divine work which he is sent to accomplish. The common distinction between success and failure breaks down completely at this point. The teaching and healing ministry as well as Jesus' suffering and death are to be understood as success. Together they constitute the victorious work of the Son of God. It would, therefore, not be correct to say that the withdrawals into the wilderness area in the first half of the Gospel indicate a retreat from success. The word success could too easily be misunderstood in a shallow sense foreign to the intention of Mark. It is more accurate to say that the withdrawals to the wilderness convey a move away from scenes describing the accomplishment of Jesus' task.

An important difference between the wilderness and the mountain passages can be observed in this respect. All wilderness passages occur in the first half of the Gospel before the turning-point of the Gospel in 8.27. They express the idea of Jesus' withdrawal from scenes where he has accomplished a part of his mission. It is striking that the two scenes related to the mountain in the first half of Mark (3.13; 6.46) disclose the same trait. In the mountain scenes after 8.27 a remarkable change occurs. The passages no longer follow descriptions of work powerfully carried out, but announcements of impending disaster. The mountain is now the place on which the most solemn affirmations about the hidden glory, the necessity and the depth of suffering are made. In the second part of the Gospel the mountain is the scene where the mystery of the humiliation of the Son of God is made explicit, while in the first part both wilderness and mountain stand as silent witnesses of this mystery which is not yet openly disclosed.

The sea passages do not permit the same conclusions. Verses 2.13 and 3.17 are the only ones which can be said to indicate a retreat from an accomplished mission. In 1.16; 4.1; 5.1, 21; 7.31 this motif is not discernible. Apparently Mark incorporates traditions which describe Jesus' activity at the sea[1] and the various accounts of the crossings of the sea are simply intended to convey an idea of Jesus' travels. It would seem, therefore, that the sea in Mark's Gospel implies complex associations. The two sea miracles show elements which make the sea a twin concept of the wilderness, and in the redactionary verses 2.13 and 3.17 Mark has used the sea in a way akin to his usage of the wilderness-place. But other traditions incorporating the sea are also included in the Gospel, and the Evangelist did not go so far in his redaction as to force them all into one concept.

(*b*) All wilderness passages in Mark imply the notion of retreat. Concerning this point the similarity to the scenes on the mountain and at the sea is even more pronounced. Regarding the mountain

[1] Bultmann, *History*, pp. 241 f.

the concept is expressed in 3.13 by the contrast of the preceding scene depicting the throng of people coming from all over Palestine and the solitude of Jesus with the chosen twelve. In 6.46 the retreat is expressly stated (ἀπῆλθεν), while in 9.2 and 13.3 the concept is underlined by the accompanying phrase κατ' ἰδίαν and the selection of the favourite three or four which is also found in 14.33. The withdrawal is also expressed in the sea passages 2.13 and 3.7 and, moreover, in the redactionary introductions which Mark has given to the two miracles on the sea (4.35; 6.45).

What is the Evangelist's intention in stating these retreats? From the foregoing discussions it is clear that the wilderness, the mountain and the sea cannot be isolated one from the other. The wilderness is thematically the dominant factor, and mountain and sea are variations dependent on the desert theme. If this is taken into account, the retreats become indications of a powerful theological thought. Jesus, after the successful performances of his teaching and healing ministry, in his withdrawals returns to the place where his mission properly began—to the desert. What happened in the story of the forty days (1.12 f.) is not merely an incident among others limited to a certain period. The Spirit did not cease to drive him to the wilderness. Rather this is the leitmotif of Jesus' whole ministry, repeated over and over again in the history which began with the baptism by John and ended at the Cross.

It would, therefore, not be correct to interpret the withdrawals as flight from success. Mark's intention is not to question the value of Christ's victory in word and deed. The exorcisms, the nature miracles, the healings and the debates are all expressions of his victory over the power of Satan, and as such they are essential to Jesus' ministry. But from the scenes of victory Jesus returns to the places which indicate his ongoing confrontation with evil. His victories over evil, as related in Mark, are not overshadowed by scepticism, and the retreats do not suggest a critical attitude towards miracles in general. But they do say that the miracles are not to be regarded as final triumphs. In them the decisive struggle takes shape, but it is not ultimately won. The scenes of triumph amongst the crowds change into the scenes of new confrontation with the evil power in solitude in order to show that the battle is still going on. For this reason the withdrawals are better understood as renewed attacks than as any form of retreat. J. M. Robinson has pointed out that the exorcism stories and the debates carry the cosmic struggle from the solitary encounter with Satan into historical settings.[1] It is possible to say that the wilderness, mountain, and sea passages refer the historical setting back to the cosmic struggle. Wilderness, mountain and sea are reminders of a deeper level of history undergirding the historically tangible events of Christ's ministry.

It is striking, moreover, that the great majority of passages connected with the wilderness, the mountain and the sea occur in the first half of the Gospel, before the turning-point in 8.27. The wilderness passages are restricted to chapters 1, 6, and 8; in 7.31 the last reference occurs to Jesus' activity at the lakeside, and regarding the mountain the characteristic difference of 9.2, 13.3 and 14.32 has already been mentioned. As Jesus' withdrawal to these places serves to point out that the final victory over Satan was not yet achieved in the miracles, Mark's plan in the arrangement of his Gospel becomes distinct. The final victory over Satan is achieved in Jesus' obedience to his destiny of suffering and death. Beginning with the first passion prediction, this theme is the centre around which the second half of the Gospel revolves. It is, therefore, no longer necessary to speak of retreats to the wilderness. The ultimate goal of the way through the wilderness is revealed in the predictions of the passion; the confrontation of the Son of man with the power of evil leads to his death. Thus, the withdrawals to desert, mountain and sea in the first half of the Gospel represent in semi-symbolic form the suffering predictions of the latter half. They establish the unity of the Gospel, linking the accounts of Jesus' public ministry with his way to the Cross. The wanderer through the wilderness is the one who is going to die. The whole success of his ministry, on the other hand, is a manifestation of the hidden power of his way through the desert as the man whose repentance is true.[2]

[1] *Op. cit.*, p. 34.
[2] Wilhelm Wrede in his famous book *Das Messiasgeheimnis in den Evangelien* (2nd ed. 1913) considered the passages dealing with Jesus' solitude and retreats as part of Mark's theory of the Messianic secret (pp. 135 f.). To Wrede the Messianic secret is a dogmatic construction designed to overcome the discrepancy between the original accounts about Jesus whose life was unmessianic in character and the belief of the Church that Jesus was made the Messiah in his resurrection (pp. 227 f.). The retreats, in Wrede's view, are

(*c*) The third element of the wilderness passages which we have observed is the strong attraction of the multitudes to Jesus and their resulting pressing out to him into the waste regions. It is striking, however, that the scenes on the mountain and at the sea hardly show the same element—the mountain not at all and the sea only in two places (3.7; 4.1). The question arises whether the analogy between the three localities breaks down at this point. A closer scrutiny of the evidence would seem to show that this is not so. While in 1.35 f. and 1.45 the wilderness is simply said to be the place to which the crowds come to seek Jesus, the pericope of the feeding of the five thousand indicates much more than this. The attraction to Jesus and the resultant move into the wilderness is clearly stated (6.33), but it is also obvious that the crowds are made witnesses of an epiphany. The feeding discloses the glory of the Son of God in the wilderness and the crowd partakes of it. It is remarkable that all stories in Mark which have the character of the epiphany are related to either wilderness, mountain or sea. The baptism and the feeding stories are located in the desert (1.9 ff., 6.30 ff., 8.1 ff.), the sea miracles, naturally, take place on the sea (4.35 ff.; 6.47 ff.), and the transfiguration is related to the mountain (9.2 ff.), while the second sea miracle is also preceded by an account of Jesus' retreat to the mountain (6.46). In the light of this evidence the impression of an attraction to Jesus in the wilderness passages assumes a different emphasis and a deeper meaning. The point is not simply that the crowds are attracted, but rather that they are made witnesses and partakers of the eschatological struggle between Jesus and evil at the places which indicate this continual fight. For that reason the mountain is the proper place for the calling of the twelve (3.13–19). They are to be companions who not only witness Jesus' fight, but also spread the same warfare, since they are charged to preach and given power to drive out demons (3.14 f.). Through them Jesus' work is continued and thus they stand equally face to face with the power of Satan. The mountain as the place of their calling is the indication of this basic condition of their mission.

---

intended to guard the secret of the Messiahship. If the discussions of this chapter have been correct, Wrede's thesis would have to be reversed. The retreats are not meant to conceal but rather to reveal Jesus' true character as they disclose the eschatological function of the Son of God to fulfil his mission in the wilderness.

VII

THE WILDERNESS IN MATTHEW AND LUKE

THE wilderness theme is a concept of considerable importance in the Second Gospel. However, a glance at a synopsis of the Gospels demonstrates that both Matthew and Luke differ from Mark with respect to this idea. The difference is quite obvious in the case of Matthew, while Luke presents a more complex picture.

1. MATTHEW

The starting-point for our discussions of the wilderness theme in Mark were, apart from the prologue, the Evangelist's remarks about the retreats to the wilderness area (1.35, 45; 6.31 f.). Matthew has omitted the accounts of a withdrawal to the wilderness given in Mark 1.35 and 1.45. At the beginning of the story of the miraculous feeding he preserves Mark 6.32 almost verbatim (Matt. 14.13), but at this place the appearance of the phrase 'wilderness-place' does not prove an appreciation of Mark's intentions on Matthew's part, as the setting of the whole story requires a scene away from human habitation. A close inspection of Matthew's rendering of the story shows either that from a lack of understanding he attempted to 'improve' upon some of Mark's seemingly obscure phrases, or that he consciously aimed at a correction of Mark's account. The crucial elements in the version of the second Evangelist—the idea of rest, the shepherd motif, the details of the green grass and of the grouping of the people—are all connected with the wilderness theme (see pp. 134–38). It cannot be coincidence that they are eliminated in Matthew's text (Matt. 14.13–21).

The wilderness theme is firmly connected with the group of narratives forming the prologue of Mark. Matthew has here retained the wilderness in his parallel accounts. But he has reduced to mere topographical remarks what to Mark was a powerful theological concept. Thus he begins his report of the activity of the Baptist by saying that John came 'preaching in the wilderness of Judea' (3.1). In comparison to Mark's account two things stand out in Matthew's text. (1) The wilderness which throughout Mark's prologue is geographically undetermined is given topographical precision by the first Evangelist.[1] What can be regarded as a gain in historical accuracy is at the same time, however, a loss of substance; the wilderness has lost its theological significance for Matthew and has become merely the designation for a certain place. (2) In Mark's prologue the Old Testament quotation has a determining quality. Whatever the prologue contains is an exegesis of the prophecy. Matthew also records Isa. 40.3 (4.3), but his account of the Baptist's preaching, appearance and baptizing cannot be understood as an immediate explication of the prophet's words. Hence, in Matthew, the connexion between the wilderness in the Isaiah quotation and the wilderness of Judea as the locality of John's activity is more mechanical and less intimate.

The narrative of Jesus' temptation begins with the statement that Jesus was 'led up . . . into the wilderness' (4.1). The expression 'led up' reflects the knowledge of the mountainous plateau of the Judean desert and is, therefore, again more geographically oriented than Mark's version. While in Mark the wilderness is the place of temptation *par excellence*, to Matthew the desert, the city of Jerusalem and the mountain are equally connected with the temptation. Since a connexion between mountain and wilderness cannot, in contrast to the second Evangelist, be traced in Matthew,[2] the three phases of the temptation must be said to have their setting in the first Gospel in three distinct localities. That is to say that none of these localities is by its own nature especially related to temptation. The words of Satan alone determine the nature of the temptation and the topographical statements simply serve as the setting for these words.

[1] This has been observed by Lohmeyer-Schmauch, *Das Evangelium des Matthäus*, 2nd ed., 1958, p. 34, and by W. Marxsen, *Der Evangelist Markus*, p. 28.

[2] W. Schmauch (*Orte der Offenbarung und der Offenbarungsort im Neuen Testament*, pp. 69 ff.) has pointed out that the mountain is particularly stressed in the first Gospel. The events of Jesus' history are flanked at the beginning and at the end by the mountain of temptation and the mountain of the last resurrection appearance and during the course of this history the mountain appears to be the place designated for teaching (5.1; 15.29).

Christ in the Wilderness

In comparing Matthew's account of the feeding of the five thousand with the Marcan version, it was asked whether the first Evangelist did not understand Mark, or whether he consciously corrected what he found in Mark's text. It would seem that Matt. 24.26 provides an answer to this question. In the apocalyptic discourse of Jesus Matthew alone records the saying 'If they say to you, "Lo, he is in the wilderness", do not go out.' The saying is readily understandable on the basis of Jewish Messianic expectations. The Messiah was expected to begin his work in the wilderness and the saying warns the Christian congregation against the danger of falling a prey to any Messianic hopes apart from the expectation of the final and completely unmistakable revelation of the Son of man (24.27). Apparently, Matthew had reasons to include this saying in the apocalyptic discourse. The Palestinian congregations to which his Gospel is addressed were surrounded by a Judaism in which the fervency of Messianic hopes was undiminished. This hope and the wilderness were, however, so much tied together that Matthew in rejecting the former also was constrained to speak out against speculations arising from the concept of the wilderness. His elimination of the most characteristic phrases in Mark's use of the wilderness theme and his attempts to blunt the edge of other Marcan passages by reducing the wilderness to a mere place name are, then, seen to be conscious efforts on his part to discard an element of Mark's work which he judged to be dangerous for the congregations in which he lived. The existence of the covenanters of Qumran and the groups which survived and continued the discipleship of John the Baptist must have been a constant temptation to Palestinian Christianity in the first century. Surrounded by these forces Matthew was unable to follow Mark's use of the wilderness tradition.

2. LUKE

In contrast to Matthew, Luke has preserved the passages in Mark which mention the retreats to the wilderness (cf. Mark 1.35, 45, with Luke 4.42; 5.16). The setting of the retreats is the same and slight alterations do not seem to be of great importance.[1] In

---

[1] Luke 4.42 does not mention Jesus' prayer as Mark 1.35 does, while Luke 5.16 adds the prayer where Mark had in 1.45 not reported it.

his account of the feeding miracle, however, Luke has not retained the emphasis on the desert setting in the introduction to the narrative. Instead he has substituted Bethsaida for Mark's wilderness (9.10). Of Mark's significant elements in this narrative he has also dropped the motifs of rest, of the shepherd and of the green grass, but he has, in a slightly different form, preserved the grouping of the people (9.10–17). One cannot help feeling that Luke was not in a position to understand the true significance of Mark's account. The fact of the preservation of Mark 1.35 and 1.45 is, therefore, likely to be due to the third Evangelist's faithfulness in the reproduction of his sources rather than to a proper appreciation of Mark's intention.

The remaining passages in Luke mentioning the wilderness seem to confirm this impression. In 1.80, at the conclusion of the stories about the infancy of the Baptist, it is said that 'the child grew and became strong in spirit, and he was in the wilderness till the day of his manifestation to Israel'. It is possible that this verse indicates a period of education in an Essene community,[1] and since the texts of Qumran show that the eschatological expectations of the covenanters were bound up with the idea of a preparation in the wilderness for the decisive event of salvation it could appear that Luke was familiar with the basic implications of the wilderness tradition. However, the continuation of 1.80 in 3.1–6 excludes this possibility. The 'day of his manifestation to Israel' (1.80) is undoubtedly the moment when 'the word of God came to John the son of Zechariah in the wilderness' (3.2). After receiving the word of God in the wilderness John is said to have gone 'into all the region about the Jordan' (3.3). There are two possible ways in which this might be taken. Either Luke meant to portray John as having received the word of God in the wilderness and subsequently leaving the wilderness region to move north along the Jordan valley.[2] The wilderness and the region about the Jordan would then be two quite distinct localities and the following quotation of Isa. 40.3–5 in 4.4–6 would involve an inconsistency on Luke's part.[3] The other possibility is that R. W. Funk

---

[1] So, e.g., A. R. C. Leaney, *The Gospel according to St Luke*, 1958, p. 91.
[2] Cf. A. Plummer, *A Critical and Exegetical Commentary on the Gospel of St Luke* (ICC), 5th ed., 1922, p. 85.
[3] K. L. Schmidt, *Der Rahmen der Geschichte Jesu*, p. 24.

is right in holding that ἔρημος is a well-established expression for a territory which includes the lower Jordan valley.[1] In this case the wilderness in 3.2 and the region about the Jordan in 3.3 would be but different wordings denoting the same locality. In both cases, however, the evidence shows that Luke has no concept of the wilderness as it is represented by Mark. In case the first explanation should be correct, it would be clear that John's activity is in no way determined by the wilderness. The wilderness would only be the place of the preparation for and the reception of the word of God, while John's characteristic mission takes places outside its limits. Should the second assumption be right, the Jordan region, viz. the wilderness, together would be the demarcation of the activity of John which in Luke is carefully distinguished from the sphere of Jesus' mission. H. Conzelmann has pointed out that in Luke the area of John's activity is set apart from the region in which Jesus works.[2] John, who in Luke is described as the last of the prophets of the old epoch (16.16), receives the word of God and works in the wilderness, while Jesus, the beginner of the new epoch, is solely associated with territory outside the circumference of John's ministry. The wilderness, then, becomes a topographical symbol for the old epoch which is superseded by Jesus. Any positive connexion between Jesus and the wilderness is hereby excluded and the report of Jesus' temptation in the wilderness, which is retained by Luke (4.1), is to be regarded as the event of transition from the old epoch to the new which starts when, after the victory over temptation, Jesus starts his work preaching 'the good news of the kingdom of God' (16.16).[3] This concept of the end of an old epoch is strengthened by the end of the Lucan version of the temptation narrative. Verse 4.13 states that after the temptation the devil departed from Jesus until an opportune time. Conzelmann has rightly stressed that this means that Jesus' life is not regarded as a temptation; 'henceforth there will be no temptations in the life of Jesus.'[4]

In view of the previous discussion of Mark's concept of the wilderness it needs no emphasis that Luke's use of the word is

[1] R. W. Funk, 'The Wilderness', *JBL* 78 (1959), p. 210.
[2] H. Conzelmann, *The Theology of St Luke*, ET, 1960, pp. 22 ff.
[3] Conzelmann, *ibid.*, p. 27.
[4] Conzelmann, *ibid.*, p. 28.

totally different. Although he did not change Mark's accounts as thoroughly as did Matthew, his understanding of the life of Jesus made it impossible for him to accept the Jewish wilderness tradition as a means of interpretation of Christ's mission, if, indeed, he was familiar with it at all.[1]

[1] For this reason, it would seem untenable when J. Mánek ('The New Exodus in the Books of Luke', *Novum Testamentum* II, 1 [1957], pp. 8–23) regards the typology of the new exodus as a dominant feature of the theology of Luke. His explanation of Luke 9.31 as an allusion to Israel's exodus seems to me unlikely in view of Luke's total theology.

INDEX OF AUTHORS

Albright, W. F., 43 n., 46 n.
Allegro, J. M., 59 n.
Anderson, R. T., 46 n.

Bach, R., 17 n.
Barr, J., 19 n.
Barrett, C. K., 76 n.
Barth, G., 13
Barth, K., 32 n.
Barth, M., 96 n.
Baur, F. C., 64 n.
Behm, J., 54 n., 84 n., 87 n.
Beyerlin, 25 n.
Boas, G., 46 n.
Bonnard, P., 62 n., 66
Boobyer, G. H., 117 n., 133 n.
Bornkamm, G., 13
Bowman, J. W., 46 n.
Brandt, W., 84 n.
Branscomb, B. H., 104 n.
Briggs, C. A., 37 n., 40 n.
Bright, J., 23 n., 24 n.
Budde, K., 46 n.
Bultmann, R., 11, 64 n., 67 n., 75 n., 76 n., 91 n., 95 n., 96 n., 97 n., 100 n., 104 n., 110 n., 111 n., 116 n., 129 n., 133 n., 136 n., 140 n.

Cadbury, J. H., 57 n.
Carlston, C. E., 116 n.
Charles, R. H., 59 n.
Colson, F. H., 53 n.
Conzelmann, H., 13, 148
Craig, C. T., 63 n., 68 n.
Cross, F. M., 59 n., 61 n.
Cullmann, O., 64 n., 96 n.

Daniélou, J., 72 n.
Daube, D., 95 n.

Delling, G., 91
Dibelius, M., 11, 12, 72 n., 96 n., 97, 104 n., 111 n., 129 n., 136 n., 138 n.
Dodd, C. H., 11 n., 75 n., 121 n.
Driver, S. R., 32 n., 33 n., 35 n.
Duhm, B., 39 n.
Dupont, J., 97 n., 100 n.

Ebeling, H. J., 105 n.
Eichrodt, W., 25
Eissfeldt, O., 24 n., 30 n., 38 n., 50 n.
Elliott-Binns, L. E., 93 n.
Euthymius, 108 n.

Farrer, A., 81 n., 125 n.
Filson, F. V., 82 n.
Flight, J. W., 46 n.
Foerster, W., 108 n., 110 n.
Frieling, R., 108 n.
Funk, R. W., 18 n., 78 n., 82, 147 f.

Galling, K., 20 n., 28
Gesenius, W., 18 n., 19 n.
Gnilka, J., 120 n., 121 n.
Goguel, M., 96 n., 116 n.
Goppelt, L., 62 n., 63 n., 64 n., 100 n.
Grant, F. C., 11 n.
Greven, H., 95 n.
Gunkel, H., 40 n., 43 n.

Haenchen, E., 57 n., 68, 71 n.
Haldar, A., 44 n.
Hanson, R. P. C., 70 n.
Held, H. J., 13
Holtzmann, H. J., 81 n.
Hort, F. J. A., 77

Index of Authors

Jackson, F. J. F., 68 n.
Jaubert, A., 59 n.
Jeremias, A., 108 n.
Jeremias, Joachim, 55 n., 56 n., 84 n., 88, 100 n., 106 n., 111 n., 114 n., 118 n., 120 n., 121 n., 135 n.
Jeremias, Johannes, 108 n.
Johnson, S. E., 79 n., 81 n., 100 n., 104 n., 111 n., 126 n., 133 n., 137 n., 138 n.
Junker, H., 38 n.

Käsemann, E., 74
Kittel, R., 55 n., 99 n.
Klostermann, E., 91 n., 111 n., 114 n.
Kraeling, C. H., 55 n., 83 n., 84 ff., 90 n.
Kraeling, E. G., 103 n.
Kraus, H. J., 38 n., 39 n., 40 n., 42 n., 43 n.

Lake, K., 57 n.
Leaney, A. R. C., 98 n., 118 n., 147 n.
Leipoldt, J., 84 n.
Lightfoot, R. H., 11 n., 77 n., 92 n., 102
Lohmeyer, E., 13, 77 n., 79 f., 81 n., 84 ff., 91 n., 92 n., 93, 95, 96 n., 97 n., 100 n., 104, 105 n., 111 n., 113, 123 n., 126 n., 133 n., 134 n., 136 n., 137 n., 138 n., 145 n.
Lohse, E., 74 n.
Lovejoy, A. O., 46 n.
Lütgert, W., 64 n.

Macgregor, G. H. C., 70 n.
Mánek, J., 62 n., 118 n., 149 n.
Manson, T. W., 120 n., 121 n.
Manson, W., 63 n., 70 n., 72 n.
Marsh, H. G., 84 n.
Marsh, J., 62 n.
Marxsen, W., 13, 78, 93 n., 104 n., 120 n., 145 n.

Masson, Ch., 120 n.
McGinley, L. T., 11 n.
Meyer, R., 93 n.
Michaelis, W., 133 n.
Michel, O., 67 n., 72 n., 74 n.
Milik, J. T., 58 n., 59 n., 60 n.
Moffatt, J., 72 n.
Molin, G., 60 n.
Moore, G. F., 84
Muilenburg, J., 50 n.

Nestle, E., 77
Noth, M., 16, 23 n., 24 n., 25 n., 30 n., 31 n., 117 n.

Oepke, A., 114 n.

Pedersen, J., 19 n., 24 n., 30, 31 n., 36 f., 42 n.
Pfeiffer, R. H., 23 n., 24 n.
Plummer, A., 63 n., 65 n., 66 n., 147 n.
Purdy, A. C., 72 n.

Quell, G., 25

Rabin, Ch., 59 n.
Rad, G. v., 16, 20 n., 25 n., 27 n., 32, 34 n., 118 n.
Rawlinson, A. E. J., 81 n., 92 n., 104 n., 138 n.
Redlich, E. B., 11 n.
Reitzenstein, R., 84 n.
Riesenfeld, H., 111 n., 116, 118 n.
Robertson, A., 63 n., 65 n., 66 n.
Robinson, H. W., 23 n., 28 n.
Robinson, J. M., 91 n., 99, 102 n., 125 n., 126 n., 130 n., 131 n., 142
Rowley, H. H., 29 n., 58 n.

Sahlin, H., 62 n., 75 n.
Schlatter, A., 64 n., 65 n.
Schmauch, W., 18 n., 62 n., 66, 99 n., 108 n., 109 n., 145 n.
Schmidt, K. L., 11, 77 f., 104 n., 147 n.
Schmithals, W., 64 n.

Index of Authors

Schniewind, J., 97 n., 100 n., 105 n., 126 n., 133 n.
Schoeps, H. J., 70 n., 71 n., 72 n., 87 n.
Schweitzer, A., 136 n.
Schweizer, E., 91 n., 95 n.
Scott, R. B. Y., 50 n.
Sellin, E., 46 n.
Simon, M., 68, 69 n., 70 n., 71 n.
Simpson, C. A., 23 n.
Stegner, W. R., 61 n.
Stendahl, K., 81 n.
Strauss, D. F., 137 n.
Streeter, B. H., 112 n., 133 n.
Sundwall, J., 79 n.

Taylor, V., 11 n., 77 n., 79, 80 n., 81 n., 92 n., 95 n., 96 n., 97 n., 98 n., 103 n., 104, 105 n., 108 n., 114 n., 116 n., 120 n., 124 n., 125 n., 126 n., 133 n., 136 n., 138 n.

Thomas, J., 84 n.
Torrey, C. C., 50 n.

Vermès, G., 59 n.
Vriezen, Th. C., 24 n., 25 n., 26 n., 28, 29 n.

Weiser, A., 16 n., 20 n., 25 n., 41 n., 48 n.
Westcott, B. F., 77
Wiebe, W., 56 n.
Williams, C. S. C., 68 n., 69 n., 70 n.
Williams, G. H., 62 n.
Wolff, H. W., 45 n., 46 ff.
Wrede, W., 142 n.
Wright, G. E., 16 n., 32 n., 34 n., 82 n.

Yates, J. E., 90

Zimmerli, W., 17 n., 49 n.

INDEX OF REFERENCES

OLD TESTAMENT

Genesis	
1.2	51
3	32 n.
9.9 ff.	26 n.
12.2 f.	28 n.
17	26 n.
22.1	35
26.3 f.	28 n.
26.8	31 n.
31.44 ff.	26 n.

Exodus	
1.11 f.	34 n.
3	23
3.1	23, 117
3.13 f.	23 f.
4.10	29
4.22 f.	28, 96
6.2	23
12.11	133
12.39	51
13.17 ff.	21
14.10 f.	29
14.19	101 n.
15.22 f.	22
15.24	29
15.25	22, 34 n.
16.2 f.	29
16.4 f., 20, 35	22
17	64 n.
17.1	22
17.2	29
17.5 f.	22
18.21	137
18.25	60
19.1 f.	117
19.4	21
19.9, 11, 16, 18	42

Exodus	
20	110
20.24	25
21.11	33 n.
23.20	80 f., 101 n.
23.23	101 n.
24	30, 110, 116 f.
24.3, 7	26 n.
24.8	138
24.12–18	111 ff.
24.16	42
24.18	99
27.21	113
32	29 f., 35
32.1	31 n.
32.4 ff.	31
32.10, 19	32
32.20	31 n.
32.25 ff.	31 n.
32.32	94
32.34	31 n., 101 n.
33	23 f.
33.2	101 n.
33.7 ff.	113
33.12 f., 16 f.	48 n.
33.19	24
34	23 f., 30, 32
34.6 f.	24
34.29	112
34.30	113

Leviticus	
16.7 ff.	98 n.

Numbers	
2.1–5.4	61
5.1–4	61
9.15	113

Numbers	
14	73
14.2 f.	29
20	64 n.
20.11 f.	40 n.
21.4–9	75
21.5	29
21.6 ff.	37 n.
21.21 ff., 33 ff.	38
27.17	135
33.14	22

Deuteronomy	
1.1	15
1.1 ff.	33
1.6–3.29	20
1.15	60
1.31	37
1.37	40 n.
3.20	33 n.
3.26	40 n.
4.21	40 n.
4.34	34, 35 n.
5.15	33 n.
6.16	35 n.
6.21 ff.	16
7.7	35
7.18	33 n.
8.2	33 n., 34 n., 35
8.3	34
8.15	36 n., 37 n.
8.16	34 n., 35
8.18	33 n.
9.4	35
9.6–21	35 n.
9.7	33 n., 35
12.9	48 n.
12.9 f.	33 n.

154

Index of References

Deuteronomy
15.5	33 n.
16.3, 12	33 n.
18.15	114
22.18	34 n.
24.9, 18, 22	33 n.
25.17, 19	33 n.
26.5 ff.	16
26.16 ff.	33 n.
27.9 f.	27, 33
29.23	42
32.7	33 n.
32.10	17, 28
32.50 ff.	40 n.

Joshua
1.13	33 n., 73
1.15	33 n.
15.61	58
21.44	33 n.
24.2 ff.	16
24.15	26 n.

Judges
2.10 ff.	38 n.
6.2	110
17.1 ff.	30

I Samuel
18.3	26 n.

II Samuel
22	42 n.

I Kings
12.27 ff.	30
17.3–6	115
18.4	110, 115
18.12	98 n.
19	117
19.4–8	115
19.5, 7	101
19.8	99, 110
19.9	115
19.9 ff.	110
19.15	99

II Kings
1.8	55 n., 83
1.9	115
2.16	98 n., 115
10.15 f.	46 n.

Job
30.3–8	37, 136

Psalms
2.7	96
11	41 f.
18.7–15	42 f.
23.1	137
29.8	41 n.
32.6	42 n.
66.6, 10 ff.	41 n.
68	43 f.
68.7 f.	48 n.
69.2	42 n.
74.13 f.	43
77.16 ff.	43
78	38 f.
80.8	41 n.
81.5–10	41 n.
88.6 f.	42 n.
91.11 ff.	100
95	40 f., 72 ff.,
99.7	41 n.
105	17 n., 37 f.
106	39 f.
106.27	49 n.
107.4 ff.	41 n.
135	37 f.
136	37 f.

Isaiah
1.2	17 n.
13.21	101 n.
32.15	52, 95
34	50 n.
34.8 ff.	37 n., 51
34.11	51
34.14	101 n.
35	50 n.
35.1 f.	51

Isaiah
35.5 ff.	52 n.
35.6 f.	51
35.9	37 n., 51
40	50
40.2	50
40.3	51, 60, 81, 83, 145
40.3–5	147
40.9	50
41.17 ff.	51
42.1	96
43.5 ff.	50
43.16 f., 19 f.	51
44.3	52, 95
44.22	89
45.18, 20 f.	51
49.6	52 n.
49.10 f.	51
50.2	51
51.3, 9 f.	51
51.11	50
51.17	129
52.7 f.	50
52.12 f.	51
53.2	52 n.
63.10 ff.	52, 95
63.14	135
64.9	19 n.

Jeremiah
2.2	28, 48 n., 96
2.2 f.	45 n.
4.23 ff.	19 n., 48 n.
9.10 f.	37 n.
10.22	37 n.
12.4	37
18.4	47
20.35	50 n.
22.6	48 n.
25.15	129
31.2	17, 48 n., 135
31.31	48 n.
32.43	48 n.

155

Index of References

Jeremiah	
33.10 ff.	48 n.
35.6 f.	46 n.
49.18	42
50.40	42

Ezekiel	
3.14	79
8.3	98 n.
16.5	17
20	48 f.
20.5 f.	28
20.23	40 n.
23.33	129
26.19 ff.	37
34	50 n.
34.5	37 n., 135
34.6	136
34.23	135

Ezekiel	
34.25	37 n., 135
34.26 f., 29	136

Daniel	
7.9	113

Hosea	
2	45
2.14	47
3.4 f.	48
5.4	47
9.10	17
11.1	16, 28, 96
11.1 ff.	45
11.5	47
12.9	16
13.4	16
13.4 f.	45 n.

Amos	
2.10	16, 47
4.6–11	47
5.25	47
9.7	16

Micah	
6.4 f.	17

Zephaniah	
2.13 f.	19 n.
2.14 f.	37 n.

Zechariah	
13.4	55 n.

Malachi	
1.3 f.	19 n.
3.1	80 f.

OLD TESTAMENT APOCRYPHA

Ecclesiasticus	
48.10	118

I Maccabees	
2.28	110
4.5	110

I Maccabees	
9.38, 40	110

NEW TESTAMENT

Matthew	
3.1	82, 145
3.3	81 n.
3.11	101 n.
3.11 f.	90
3.14 f.	94
4.1	145
4.1 ff.	97
4.3	145
4.6	100 n.
4.11	100
5.1	145
11.7	104
11.10	81 n.
14.13	104
14.13–21	144
15.29	145
15.33	104
17.2	112
18.12	110

Matthew	
23.37 ff.	94
24.26	58
24.26 f.	146

Mark	
1.1–13	77 ff., 130
1.2 f.	80 ff.
1.3 f.	103
1.4–8	82 ff.
1.5	132
1.9–11	90 ff., 143
1.11	114, 117
1.12 f.	96 ff., 129 f., 141
1.12	103
1.13	123, 131
1.14 f.	125
1.14	102
1.16–20	125

Mark	
1.16	140
1.21–45	105
1.12–34	105
1.23–26	130
1.23	131 n.
1.25	126
1.35–39	104
1.35 f.	143
1.35	103 ff., 128, 144, 146
1.36 ff.	107
1.36	131
1.39	130
1.45	103 ff., 124, 143 f., 146
2.1–12	124 f., 127
2.13	124 f., 127 f., 132, 139 f., 141

Index of References

Mark		Mark		Mark	
2.14	124, 127, 132	6.30–8.26	119	9.5 f.	131
2.27	131 n.	6.30–44	133	9.7	96 n.
3.1–5	125	6.30–33	104 f., 143	9.11–13	111 n., 118
3.1	131 n.	6.31 f.	103 ff., 119, 144	9.18	131
3.5	122, 131 n.	6.32	127	9.25	126
3.6 f.	124 f., 127 f.	6.33	143	9.28	120
3.7–12	125	6.35	103 ff.	9.34	123, 131
3.7 f.	132, 139, 141, 143	6.39	103	10.2	131
3.11 f.	130	6.45–50	126 f.	10.7, 9	131 n.
3.12	126	6.45	109, 141	10.13	123
3.13–19	125, 143	6.46	107 ff., 118, 128, 139 ff., 143	10.28	131
3.13	109, 118, 139 ff.	6.47	143	10.32 f.	94
3.15	130	6.48	108	10.37	123, 131
3.16	131	6.52	122, 131	10.38	91 f.
3.17	140	6.53	127	10.45	94
3.22–30	130	7.1	94	11.1	57 n., 108
3.22	94, 99, 130	7.11, 15	131 n.	11.23	108
3.23 ff.	122	7.17–23	122	11.30	92
3.29	91	7.18	131	12.1 ff.	122
3.30	130 n.	7.20	131 n.	12.1	131 n.
4.1–34	120 ff.	7.31	140, 142	12.15	131
4.1	140, 143	7.33	120, 124	13.3 ff.	119
4.11	132	8.1–10	133 n., 143	13.3	108 f., 124, 119 f., 139, 141 f.
4.15	99	8.4	78 n., 103 ff.	13.14	110
4.26	131 n.	8.10	127	13.34	131 n.
4.35–41	126 f., 143	8.11	131	13.35, 37	134
4.35	141	8.13	127	14.12	138
4.39	125	8.17	122, 131	14.13	131 n.
4.40	131	8.21	131	14.18	108
5.1	140	8.27	128, 140, 142	14.22	138 n.
5.2	110, 131 n.	8.31	111, 118, 124	14.24	94
5.8	131 n.	8.32	118	14.25	138
5.11	110	8.33	123, 131	14.26	108
5.13	101 n., 126	8.34–9.1	109	14.27	139
5.21	127, 132, 140	8.34–38	111	14.28	94
5.37, 40	120, 124	8.35	123 f.	14.32–42	107 f., 119, 128 ff.
6.7–13	133	9.1	111	14.32	139, 142
6.7	130	9.2–8	110 ff., 143	14.33	119, 141
6.12	106	9.2	109, 124, 119 f., 139, 141 f.	14.34, 37 f., 40	134
6.14–29	133			14.41	134 f.
6.14 ff.	83			14.50	123
				14.71	131 n.

157

Index of References

Mark
16.5	113
16.7	94

Luke
1.80	105, 147
3.1–6	147 f.
3.3	82
3.4	81 n.
3.16 f.	90
4.1–13	97
4.1	148
4.4–6	147
4.10 f.	100 n.
4.13	100, 148
4.42	106, 146
5.16	104, 146
7.27	81 n.
8.13	123
8.29	105, 110
9.10–17	147
9.29	112
9.31	118, 149 n.
14.4	110
15.4	105
16.16	148

John
1.28	82
3.13 f.	75 f.
3.23	82
6.31–33	137
6.31 f., 35	76
7.33	75
11.54	75
12.32 f.	75
14.2	75
20.12	113

Acts
2.22, 43	71 n.
4.4	121
5.12	71 n.
6.13 f.	68
7	68 ff.
8.4 f.	106 n.
13.17–25	68 n.
13.24	93
14.3	71 n.
15.12	71 n.
21.38	57

Romans
6.3	64
7.7	66

I Corinthians
6.12–20	66
6.12	64
7.31	67
10.1–13	63 ff., 73 f.
10.2	88
10.14–22	66
10.23	64
11.25	138
11.29	65

II Corinthians
3.4–18	68 n.
3.12–18	112
5.17	67
11.26	67 n.

Galatians
3.27	64
5.17	66

I Timothy
1.10	105 n.

II Timothy
4.2	106 n.

Hebrews
2.1–3	72
2.5	74
3.7–4.13	72 ff.
6.4–6	72
11.13 ff.	74
11.38	110
13.14	74

NON-BIBLICAL SOURCES

Assumption of Moses
3.11	69 n.

I Enoch
28.1	54 f.
29.1	54 f.

JOSEPHUS *Antiquities*
XX, 97–99	57

JOSEPHUS *De bello Judaico*
I, 36	110
II, 254–64	56 f.
VI, 351	57
VII, 438	57

Martyrdom of Isaiah
2.8–12	54 f.
2.8	110

PHILO *De Decalogo*
I, 2	53
II, 10–13	53
III, 14	54
IV, 15–17	54

QUMRAN CD
2.15	59 n.
6.5	59
6.19	58
7.6	60
10.2	60
19.35–20.1	60
20.12	58

Index of References

QUMRAN		1 QS		Test. Levi	
CD		1.24 ff.	59	4.3	113
20.13 ff.	60	2.21 ff.	60	4.5	112
20.17	59 n.	5.1	58		
20.23	59	5.8	59	Test. Judah	
20.26	60	5.14	58	24.1	112
		6.15	58 f.		
1 QM		8.12–16	60	Test. Zebulon	
1.2	59	9.19	60	9.8	113
7.3–7	61	10.20, 23	58		

www.ingramcontent.com/pod-product-compliance
Lightning Source LLC
Chambersburg PA
CBHW072143160426
43197CB00012B/2221